Study Skills for Psychology Students

Study Skills for Psychology Students

Jennifer Latto and Richard Latto

Open University Press

Open University Press
McGraw-Hill Education
McGraw-Hill House
Shoppenhangers Road
Maidenhead
Berkshire
England
SL6 2QL

email: enquiries@openup.co.uk
world wide web: www.openup.co.uk

and Two Penn Plaza, New York, NY 10121-2289, USA

First published 2009

A catalogue record of this book is available from the British Library

ISBN 10: 0-335-22909-3 (pb)   0-335-22910-7 (hb)
ISBN 13: 978-0-335-22909-3 (pb)   978-0-335-22910-9 (hb)

Library of Congress Cataloging-in-Publication Data
CIP data applied for

Typeset by RefineCatch Limited, Bungay, Suffolk
Printed in the UK by Bell and Bain Ltd, Glasgow

Cartoons drawn by Adam Paxman

The McGraw·Hill Companies

For Georgina Brennan, Julia Henderson and Steve McArdle

Contents

Skills for Successful Study series

Skills for Successful Study is an exciting new discipline-orientated study skills series that will benefit students by drawing on examples that will speak directly to them about the challenges and successes within their own study environments. Each book will support the student throughout their course: from the trepidation of beginning to study, through to becoming an expert learner, and onward to planning a career.

A free careers website is also available, at www.openup.co.uk/psychology success

Other titles in the series

Scullion and Guest, *Study Skills for Nursing and Midwifery Students*
More new titles coming soon!

Series editor's preface

Study Skills cover all those abilities that make it possible to cope with the demands of academic and professional pursuits. For people just embarking on a course of study they include being able to deal with all the intellectual, emotional and social challenges that are part of the day-to-day demands of being a student. Beyond the skills involved in coping are those that enable students to do well in their chosen disciplines. These embrace much more than the ability to memorize or understand the topics of study, reaching into time management, ethics and the personal and interpersonal upheavals that are often such an important part of the student's life.

The study skills that are mastered at university, or for some people earlier when studying at school, are central to what everyone has to offer as a graduate and/or professional. Some people would even suggest that the main contribution of a university degree is to provide a person with the skills for studying. It is these skills that will help the person through the rest of their career.

Studying is a skill that can be mastered like many others, by first understanding the process then by developing appropriate habits through active involvement. Yet whilst there are some aspects of the process that are common to all forms of study there are often important facets of any particular area of study that demand special skills. Further, even when the skills may be relevant across a number of different disciplines it is usually easier to understand what is required by embedding consideration of them within the specific topic.

This series of books is therefore being published with guidance on how to be an effective student within each of a series of specific domains. By dealing with study skills in relation to the area of study it is possible to ensure that the examples are directly pertinent to the student of that area, rather than being general exhortations. The books thus complement the many other publications available on such general topics as essay writing or taking examinations.

The focus on particular areas of study also enables the authors to follow the particular educational trajectory from the early entry into college or university right through to becoming a recognised professional in the chosen discipline. It allows the authors to draw on examples that speak directly to students about issues in their own lives. It also enables the books to identify particular topics that are of special significance for any given discipline.

This series therefore provides a valuable resource to all students that they can draw on as a friend and guide throughout their course of study and beyond.

David Canter
Series Editor
University of Liverpool

Introduction: why you need this handbook and how to use it

Psychology is a multi-disciplinary subject which studies the most intrinsically interesting and important topic of all: human behaviour. This is both its great strength and its great challenge. The evidence on which it draws ranges from the qualitative and descriptive approaches of some of the social sciences to the laboratory based and highly technical. As a student, you will have to come to terms with this fascinating but often challenging spectrum of methodologies and techniques. It is a stimulating, sometimes daunting, but always rewarding task, which will leave you with a wide range of knowledge and skills offered by no other degree.

Over the years, many psychology graduates have confided to us, having walked across the stage to receive their degrees, that it was only since they had really got down to work for their final exams that they had realized what a fascinating subject psychology is, and how many applications it has in everyday life. The object of this book is to bring this revelation forward so that you can make the most of our insights and advice, both to enjoy studying for your degree and to achieve more successful outcomes.

Psychology is one of the most popular undergraduate degree choices and is taught in a wide variety of universities and colleges. This handbook provides an introduction, guide and reference book for you to use at all stages in your study of psychology.

In Chapter 1, we begin by giving you a brief introduction to psychology and psychological thought, which has fascinated and intrigued us both throughout our careers. We then give you a brief starter guide to the conventions and structures of higher education. Chapter 1 also provides an indication of the resources likely to be available to you at your university or college, and how to use them to best effect to make a success of your time there. In the end, what you learn is up to you. We aim to give you a toolkit for tackling both the knowledge and skills which make up the components of a degree in psychology that you can expect to encounter, and references to further sources of information and advice.

In Chapter 2, we provide support for handling the many different kinds of input you will receive during your degree; both from reading books, **journals** and websites, and from formal teaching such as lectures, seminars and tutorials. We discuss learning in groups, learning through experience in a whole range of work situations, and how to make good use of personal development profiling. We also offer advice on how to stay on top of your rapidly accumulating store of knowledge.

Information technology plays a vital part in working for a psychology degree and we therefore devote the whole of Chapter 3 to making the most of the help it can provide.

During your course you will acquire a wide range of knowledge and useful skills, and you will be required to demonstrate them in many different kinds of assessment task. In Chapter 4 we give you our advice, based on many years of teaching students in a variety of contexts, on how to cope with essays, practical reports, presentations, posters, seminar contributions and, last but not least, examinations.

Most psychology courses have an individual research-based dissertation or project in the final year, which carries a considerable proportion of final degree marks. We devote the whole of Chapter 5 to this task, which can seem rather daunting, but, if it goes well, will form one of the most rewarding parts of the course and give you the chance to explore something of particular interest to you in considerable depth.

Chapter 6 considers eventual careers. The roles of the British Psychological Society and Regulation of Practising Psychologists by the Health Professions Council are discussed. Thoughts about postgraduate courses in psychology, practising as an applied psychologist (in the UK or abroad) and getting your first post, whether as a psychologist or not, are shared.

Detailed appendices provide important guides to referencing, psychological **acronyms**, and glossaries of common psychological and statistical terms, which you can refer to quickly while you are working. As you read through the book, the first reference in each chapter to terms that are explained in the main glossary (Appendix 4) is in bold. Look them up if you are not sure exactly what they mean. (Appendix 4 also contains details of some of the main terms that, while they are not mentioned in this book, are likely to crop up during your psychology studies.)

On the associated website (www.openup.co.uk/psychologysuccess), you will find regularly updated information about careers in many different aspects of psychology, with descriptions of what they entail and information about training, with a whole range of useful 'click on' website addresses giving further details to take you on to the next stage.

How to use this book

1 Read the book from cover to cover, ideally before you embark upon your degree. It will give you a very good idea of what the experience of a psychology degree is like, and the different challenges you will encounter.
2 As the various milestones come up: first days at university, first tutorial, first experience of university teaching, first visit to the learning resources centre, first attempts to get to grips with the IT system, first assessment, first thoughts about a career, and then your project, you will find a relevant section to help you through.
3 For advice on specific issues during the course, use it as a reference book by consulting the contents page or the index. Each chapter is divided into carefully labelled sections to help you locate advice on specific matters.
4 Study how we have presented **references**, quotations, figures and tables. We have used the American Psychological Association (APA) conventions throughout as this is the most widely used system in psychology and you will be using it, or something very similar, in your coursework. Try to become familiar with these formats and use the book as a presentation guide for your own work.

The book also includes:

- many diagrams and figures
- exercises for practising certain specific skills
- tips for quick reference help
- advice from our own students
- examiners' thoughts
- cartoons for light relief
- TOMtips (see below).

TOMtips are a particular feature of the book. They are there to encourage you to use your **theory of mind** (and here is an example of the convention throughout the book that things in bold indicate that they are in the Glossary in Appendix 4).

The importance of theory of mind (TOM) was nicely expressed at the start of the twentieth century: "Success in life rests upon one small gift – the secret of entry into another man's mind to discover what is passing there" (Henry Seton Merriman, 1901).

The subject of investigation by psychologists from a variety of theoretical persuasions, theory of mind is a powerful tool for flourishing in all those situations – such as presentations, exams and interviews – where we are trying to impress other people. Considering what your audience is thinking and feeling makes it easier to achieve the outcomes you desire.

In conclusion

No book of this kind can guarantee success: only your own efforts can achieve that, but by offering you the experience and advice gleaned from our students and our own careers, we offer you a powerful launching pad for your efforts.

You are now starting on a new journey in psychology, and this book should help you to both enjoy it and make a success of it. We hope the advice we offer here will enable you to do well, but remember that the purpose is not simply to get a degree but to enjoy learning about psychology and acquiring new skills. As Henry Miller put it: "One's destination is never a place but rather a new way of looking at things" (1957, p. 25).

1

First things first

This chapter will help orientate you to the discipline of psychology, and to find your way around your university or college.

1.1 About psychology

What is psychology?

One important and useful thing to think about for starters: psychology is a fast-evolving science and what you will be studying is only our current understanding of human behaviour. The state of our knowledge progresses through observations, which give rise to theories, which lead to predictions. We then attempt to test these predictions through **experiments** or further systematic observations, which may confirm the predictions or lead us to revise the theory. This, in very simple terms, is the scientific model (see Figure 1.1).

Experiments either confirm or contradict the theory, and lead us to modify it to accommodate our new information, which leads to more experiments. The position has been excellently summarized as 'the Endless Search' by Donald Broadbent, who taught both of us.

> We end then upon a note of doubt, with no certainty about the beliefs which future psychologists will hold. This is as it should be. Nobody can grasp the

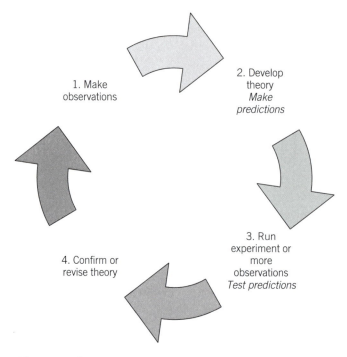

Figure 1.1. The scientific model.

nature of things from an armchair, and until fresh experiments have been performed we do not know what their results will be. The confident dogmatisms about human nature which fall so readily from pulpits, newspaper editorials, and school prize-givings are not for us. Rather, we must be prepared to live with an incomplete knowledge of behaviour but with confidence in the power of objective methods to give us that knowledge some day.

(Broadbent, 1961, p. 200)

Take dreaming, for example. Why do we dream? In the 1950s, Kleitman observed that there are periods of **rapid eye movements** (REM) during sleep, and that if the sleeper is woken during these episodes they are likely to report dreams (Aserinsky & Kleitman, 1953). Freud (1991) thought that dreams were a product of the brain working through the events and emotions of the previous day, and trying to absorb and come to terms with them. A more pragmatic explanation based on information processing theory sees dreams as analogous to clearing a memory store by processing memories at an unconscious level, preparing us for new experiences the following day. Paul McCartney picked up this idea in his album entitled "Memory Almost Full" (McCartney, 2007). There is even some evidence that sleep helps recently learnt material become consolidated into memory (Maquet et al., 2000; Born, Rasch & Gais, 2006)

Waking people constantly during REM sleep causes them to become very irritable and to function less efficiently. This could appear to reinforce either theory (or indeed neither, as people woken constantly during the night are likely to become very irritable) so further experiments are called for, and so the research goes on.

Of course it gets more complicated than this. Different groups of psychologists come at behaviour from their own theoretical standpoints, just like the people trying to explore the reason for dreaming.

Different approaches to psychology

The idea of psychology as an evolving science can be illustrated, in very broad terms, by summarizing some of the main approaches that have been adopted during its historical development.

Behaviorism

The approach to psychology developed from Ivan Pavlov's experiments in 1903 with dogs, which learned to salivate when they heard a bell that they had come to associate with the appearance of food. Behaviorists (note the American spelling) argue, and have demonstrated to some extent, that humans operate on a very simple **conditioning** model, and that behaviour can be modified by rewarding or punishing particular behaviours to increase or eliminate them. Behaviorism is based on the idea that we can only meaningfully study externally visible behaviour and that all else is valueless speculation. A person's behaviour is interpreted in terms of their learning history, particularly the patterns of reward and punishment they have experienced. It was developed by John B. Watson (1878–1958), E. Thorndike (1874–1949), B.F. Skinner (1904–1990) and others in America. Watson demonstrated **empirical** evidence for **classical conditioning** in the case of a boy called Little Albert, whom he trained to be afraid of a white rat by associating its appearance with an unpleasant stimulus. While no longer supported in its purist form, it has nevertheless proved a valuable tool in studying animal behaviour in laboratory situations and describing human behaviour in simple situations. This technique has been extensively exploited in advertising – for example, where the repeated association of an arbitrary positive stimulus, such as a beautiful woman, with an emotionally neutral object, such as a car, results in the latter coming to elicit the warm feelings associated with the former.

Biological

(Also known as physiological psychology.)

This approach concentrates on studying the activity of the nervous system, especially the brain, the action of hormones and other chemicals, and genetics, on the assumption that behaviour is largely shaped by biological processes. This approach analyses how biology shapes mental processes and behaviour – for example, how the brain controls movement, receives information from the senses or processes language. It was developed by Karl Lashley (1890–1958), who identified the role of the cortex in memory, James Olds (1922–1976), who discovered the 'reward systems' in the brain, and Donald Hebb (1904–1985), who studied the contribution of neurons to learning.

Cognitive

Cognitive psychology studies how people absorb, mentally represent and store information. It models internal mental processes such as perception, attention, memory, language and problem solving, and had its foundations in **Gestalt** psychology. Cognitive psychologists are interested in how people understand, diagnose and solve problems, i.e. the mental processes that mediate between stimulus and response. Wilhelm Wundt (1832–1920), who, together with William James (1842–1910), is seen as the father of psychology, sought to investigate the immediate experiences of consciousness (including feelings, emotions, volitions and ideas) mainly explored through **introspection** (i.e. the self-examination of conscious experience by objective observation of one's consciousness). Hermann von Helmholtz (1821–1920), another early psychologist with a background in the experimental sciences, is known for his theories of visual perception, colour vision, the sensation of tone and perception of sound. These psychologists distinguished themselves from much earlier philosophers like Renée Descartes (1596–1650), who speculated about the nature of the mind, but did not conduct experiments. Modern cognitive psychology has led to developments in human factor research in design and engineering – for example, the creation of computer keyboards, flight simulators and control panels – and to **cognitive behavioural therapy (CBT)**, now a major treatment in clinical psychology.

Cognitive neuroscience

This is a recent development bringing together cognitive psychology (which traditionally did not worry too much about underlying neural processes) with neuropsychology, which examines the link between the brain and behaviour, using evidence from the effects of brain damage on cognitive processes. Cognitive science exploits the exciting recent developments in brain imaging techniques, such as functional Magnetic Resonance Imaging (fMRI), trans-cranial magnetic stimulation (TMS) and other electrical recording procedures. Important recent examples include the discovery of mirror neurons, which mimic the behaviour of the person being observed, and the neural evidence for a distinction between perception for recognizing people and things, and perception for manipulating things and moving around in the world.

Developmental

Developmental psychologists chart the changes in behaviour and mental processes that occur over the entire human life span, and try to understand the causes and effects. They examine **quantitative** changes that can be measured –

such as increases in memory span – and **qualitative** changes – where different strategies appear to come into play, such as the appearance of a **theory of mind**. The focus of the work of Jean Piaget (1896–1980) was the qualitative description of the stages in children's cognitive development.

Evolutionary

This approach stems from the work of Charles Darwin (1809–1882) and views the behaviour of animals and humans as the result of evolution through **natural selection**. It is particularly concerned with the origins of aspects of social behaviour, such as the selection of a mate and friendship patterns (Robin Dunbar (1947–)), and in the adaptive behaviour that enabled our early ancestors to survive (Richard Dawkins (1941–)).

Humanistic

Here, behaviour is seen as determined primarily by an individual's choice as to how to act, dictated by their unique perceptions of the world. Carl Rogers (1902–1987) postulated that people have an innate tendency to develop towards their highest potential, or 'self-actualize', and personal construct theory stems from his work. Abraham Maslow (1908–1970) developed his widely quoted concept of a hierarchy of needs underlying motivation (Figure 1.2), which has had

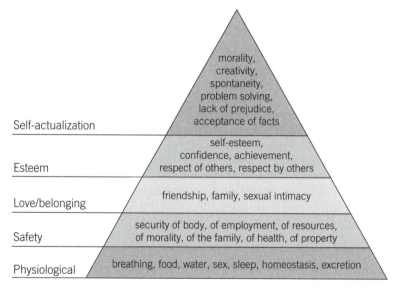

Figure 1.2. Maslow's hierarchy of needs.

considerable influence on modern organizational psychology – for example, in satisfaction questionnaires.

Psychodynamic

Rooted in the work of Sigmund Freud (1856–1939), this approach assumes that behaviour reflects the mostly unconscious conflicts between the id (the seat of our basic drives and impulses, which operates on the 'pleasure principle'), the ego (which regulates these impulses according to the restrictions imposed by society, or the 'reality principle') and the superego (which acts as the 'conscience' and tries to chart a course through the middle). His ideas, and those of his followers such as Alfred Adler (1870–1937) and Carl Jung (1875–1961), were very influential in the development of **psychoanalysis**. More recently, Melanie Klein (1882–1960) extended these ideas in working therapeutically with children, and Hans Eysenck (1916–1997) attempted to put extraversion and introversion on a more scientific footing by developing tests such as the Maudsley Personality Inventory to measure this aspect of personality more systematically.

Psychometrics

The science of psychological assessment has its origins in Ancient China and is based on the recognition that future behaviour could be predicted from a few indicative measures. Francis Galton (1822–1911), often seen as the father of psychometrics, and Karl Pearson (1857–1936), Charles E. Spearman (1863–1945) and Raymond Cattell (1905–1998) developed the statistical techniques behind modern psychometrics. Alfred Binet (1857–1911) created the first intelligence tests to identify learning difficulties during the growth of compulsory education in France. Tests fall into two main categories: knowledge-based tests, where there are right and wrong answers, including tests of ability aptitude, competence and attainment; and person-based tests, which differentiate between individual attributes, including tests of personality and attitude. Four basic principles underlie psychometric tests: **reliability**, **validity**, **standardization** and **bias**. They are widely used in education and employment today.

Social

Social psychologists are interested in the ways in which people influence one another, for example in the area of racial prejudice. The famous Stanford prison experiment led by Philip Zimbardo (1973) was a psychological study of human responses to captivity and its behavioural effects on both authorities and inmates in prison. Undergraduate volunteers played the roles of both guards and inmates, and rapidly adapted to their roles, stepping beyond the boundaries of what had been predicted, and leading to dangerous and psychologically damaging situations. One-third of the guards were judged to have exhibited 'genuine' sadistic tendencies, while many prisoners were emotionally traumatized and two had to be removed from the experiment early. In another well-known experiment, Stanley Milgram (1933–1984) demonstrated the willingness of participants in a study to obey an authority figure who instructed them to perform acts that conflicted with their conscience, and continue to deliver apparently increasingly painful electric shocks to others (Milgram, 1963).

As you can see, psychologists, both historically and today, approach behaviour and mental processes in many different ways. Let us take the study of abnormal behaviour, for example. On the one hand there is the School of Psychoanalysis and on the other, there are the Behaviorists, and they would set about treatment in a totally different way. Then there are also the **psychopharmacologists**, who view mental problems in the same way as physical problems and as therefore treatable with drugs. The interesting thing is that all these approaches work in different contexts and are sometimes used in conjunction with each other. They offer explanations but they use different languages or **levels of explanation** and so may be useful in different situations.

In many areas of psychology, therefore, there are two or more competing theories in existence and the jury is still out on which is the right one. You may even find that different lecturers argue enthusiastically for very different answers to the same question. This can be both challenging and frustrating, but it also makes the subject fun: you have the chance to consider them for yourself rather than just learning and regurgitating ideas.

Exercise 1.1 Some significant psychologists

Try looking up some other significant psychologists (listed below) and see if you can work out where they fit into this historical perspective. Use the internet, or the dictionaries listed in Appendix 6.

- Allport, Gordon (1897–1967)
- Asch, Solomon (1907–1996)
- Bartlett, Frederic (1886–1969)
- Broadbent, Donald (1926–1993)
- Bruner, Jerome SE. (1915–)
- Chomsky, Noam (1928–)
- Ellis, Albert (1913–2007)
- Fechner, Gustav (1801–1887)
- Festinger, Leon (1919–1989)
- Fodor, Jerry (1935–)
- Freud, Anna (1895–1982)
- Gregory, Richard (1923–)
- Kahneman, Daniel (1934–)
- Kleitman, Nathaniel (1895–1999)
- Kohler, Wolfgang (1887–1967)
- Marr, David (1945–1980)
- Tajfel, Henri (1919–1982)
- Vygotsky, Lev (1896–1934)

So psychology is an evolving science, and as a science it requires an evidence base, but it is a young science and, like all adolescents, is both strongly influenced by its early environment and also developing and changing fast.

Degrees in psychology

Psychology is one of the most popular undergraduate degree subjects, but the degree can take a number of forms. It is essential to check that the course you apply for carries **Graduate Basis for Registration (GBR)** if there is any possibility that you might wish to become a professional psychologist (see the section on this on page 169). Different degree structures include the following.

- Single honours: psychology is the main subject taught, but there may be sub-sidiaries, particularly in the first year.
- Combined/joint honours: psychology is only one of the subjects that contribute to the degree. This may be harder work in that you have to cope with the language and conventions of two different subjects, and with two academic departments that may operate rather differently, and you will have fewer psychology options in the third year.
- Major/minor: two subjects, of which psychology must be the major to have GBR status.
- Sandwich: one year of the course, usually the penultimate, is spent on a psychology-related placement.
- Foundation degree: two year full time equivalent course without GBR, which can lead into an honours degree.

The language of psychology

Like most academic subjects psychology has a language all its own, containing many **acronyms** and a good deal of jargon. Some of this jargon uses words in everyday use but with a slightly different meaning. This is not done to confuse you (though it may well do so) but because, to share ideas effectively in psychology, we need to have exact definitions of the words we use. So 'constancy', a word we are all familiar with in everyday life, has a very specific meaning in psychology. It refers to the very remarkable ability we have to see something as unchanging even when the stimulus generating the perception changes radically – for example, when an object rotates or moves away from us. The sooner you can start to familiarize yourself with the most common terms the better. If you continually have to look things up, the conversation will have moved on before you have established what is being discussed. This tendency to talk in a kind of code is not malicious or probably even deliberate – it just saves time when specialists talk to each other and is not unique to psychology.

Some of the more common and more confusing terms are defined in the Glossary (see Appendix 4) and there is a list of the most common acronyms and abbreviations in Appendix 3.

Exercise 1.2 Definition of specialist terms

The definitions of common terms in psychology and higher education found in the Glossary (Appendix 4) are arranged so that you can cover up either the term or the definition. Try testing yourself on them.

Many textbooks also have very useful glossaries defining the jargon words used in their particular area, and there are some very useful dictionaries and encyclo-paedias of psychology, which are listed under 'Further reading' in Appendix 6.

1.2 How your university or college works

Tip: Preparing for freshers' week

➢ It is worth reading this section carefully before arriving for your first week (often called freshers' week), which can otherwise be an overwhelming assault on your information-processing capacity.

Higher education institutions are very different places from schools and they are often very different from each other, so do not rely too much on your friend at another university or college for advice on how yours works. However, there are some common factors that they usually share. Most important, they tend to be large places, with thousands of people of all ages studying and researching together. So they are like substantial towns with a complex structure and government system. Typically you will come across four parts: your department; the central administration; the students' union; and, unless you are living at home, halls of residence or colleges, which provide your accommodation.

The department

This will either be clearly labelled as the Department/School/Institute of Psychology/Applied Psychology/Experimental Psychology or will be part of a larger grouping such as the School of Health and Behavioural Sciences. As you can see from this plethora of names there is no common pattern, but somewhere in your university there will be a group of staff whose job it is to deliver the programme on which you are enrolled. It is these people who will be your most important contacts. They will teach you, assess you, and provide academic and personal guidance. You will probably be allocated one particular staff member as your personal tutor with whom you will usually have some formal contact, but most importantly they are the person to whom you can go if you need informal advice or help. In some universities personal tutors also teach their tutees – for example, in first-year tutorials; in others, they simply have a general guidance role. As with all human endeavours, though less so than most, there will be something of a hierarchy among the departmental staff, with a head of department responsible for all the teaching and research in the department and someone with a title like 'Director of Undergraduate Teaching' or 'Course Leader' (or something totally unrecognizable), who has overall responsibility for your degree programme. These people become very important if you have a more serious problem. Departments are also commonly grouped into faculties (psychology will normally be in a faculty of science or medicine or health). You may come across faculties if you have problems, but their main function is normally in financial and strategic planning for the university, and they typically feature less in student life than departments or the central administration.

Central services

Most universities now handle much of the administration for student matters centrally. Typically, this will include all financial matters, like fee collection, scholarships and bursaries, the running of formal examinations, the allocation of accommodation, careers advice, health services, library and information technology (about which we have a great deal to say in Chapter 3), disciplinary and appeals procedures, and, of course, car parking. The most reliable advice is usually obtained by going direct to the central office concerned, although your tutor will be able to point you in the right direction. The overall head of the university will usually, and confusingly, be called the Vice-Chancellor (VC). (The Chancellor is a figurehead, rather like a queen or king, who officiates at degree ceremonies.) You may receive a morale-raising address from the Vice-Chancellor on your arrival, but unless you are very badly behaved or a sabbatical officer in the students' union you are unlikely to see them again until you graduate.

Registration

The process of signing up for the modules (see page 17) you will be taking in the current year is very important and may be organized centrally, particularly if your proposed study plan involves modules from more than one department. As with so much else at university, you will be given guidance, but the ultimate responsibility to register correctly is yours. So make sure you find out how this is done (often on the web nowadays) and that you have ticked the right boxes.

The students' union

This is an organization that has its own accommodation, and a management that is run by students and is largely independent of the university administration. There will be a number of sabbatical officers who are elected students paid for one year at the end, or sometimes in the middle, of their degree course. Their resources and functions vary between universities, but they will always be a useful source of independent help and advice if you have problems, as well as providing an important social focus. The students' union also acts as a negotiating body with the university, on behalf of students. Each individual students' union is a member of the National Union of Students (NUS), which, as the name implies, acts as a national negotiating body and pressure group. Both local and national union activities are useful training grounds for politicians, and all recent cabinets have included several ministers who have cut their teeth in this way.

If you get into difficulties with the university the students' union will be able to advise you (see 'What to do if things go wrong', page 19).

Accommodation

Unless you choose to live at home, most universities will take responsibility for helping you find accommodation. In your first year, many will try to guarantee a place for you in student accommodation in halls of residence or colleges, and will have an accommodation agency to help you find somewhere to live in subsequent years. Structures vary so much between universities that it is impossible to offer sensible general advice here, but finding somewhere that is both convenient and pleasant to live in, and conducive to effective academic work, is a vital factor in a successful university career.

Tip: Planning ahead

➢   Plan where you are going to live in your second and third year carefully and well ahead of time, perhaps with a group of other students.

The language of higher education

Like psychology itself, higher education is prone to jargon. A few of the most important terms are explained in the accompanying box.

Terms associated with your degree that you may come across

Credit

The weight given to a particular module (see below). Typically, you will have to obtain 120 credits to pass a year of your degree programme. Different universities use the credit system in different ways. So a standard module may be 15 credits, in which case you have to pass 8 modules a year, or 12 credits in which case you have to pass 10 modules a year. You may also be offered 'half modules', 'double modules' and even, perhaps for your third-year research module, 'triple modules', which will have their credit value assigned accordingly.

   Make sure you are registered for modules that will earn you the right number of credits.

Level

Modules (see below) are usually allocated to a particular level of study. So the first third of the course (year 1 if you are a full-time student) will comprise Level 1 modules.

Module

A module is essentially a short course on a particular topic (memory, statistics, etc.) at a particular level. An important component of the degree may be covered by modules at several levels, and access to the modules at higher levels may be conditional on passing earlier ones. A module will normally be self-contained, with its own assessment generating a mark at the end. Modules vary in the way they are taught, and use different patterns of lectures, seminars, tutorials and practicals. Towards the end of the course they may not really be taught at all, but will still result in an important mark. For example, many universities have an optional 'dissertation' module in the third year for which you write an extended essay on a topic of your choice, and you may get little more than some general guidance and comments on a first draft. Most importantly, modules can vary in size. This will be indicated by the number of credits (see above) you receive for passing it. Each module will have a formal *module specification*, which will be publicly available and gives its formal structure, aims, intended learning outcomes and associated assessment tasks.

Programme

A name often given to the overall degree course you are taking. It will consist of a set of compulsory and optional modules. Each programme has a formal *programme specification*, which will be publicly available and gives its formal structure.

Oxbridge

Oxford and Cambridge have a slightly different structure for achieving these functions, with a much greater emphasis on the colleges for providing pastoral support and accommodation, library, IT, and social and sporting facilities. Colleges also have a greater responsibility for tutorial-based (or supervision-based) teaching, progress monitoring and disciplinary procedures. However, there is also a departmental structure that provides the bulk of the teaching, and a central administration that serves a similar function as in other universities.

Scottish universities

The Scottish university system differs from the English one in three very important ways.

1 An undergraduate degree is normally four years (not including a sandwich year).
2 Fee arrangements for Scotland are different.[1] There are normally no tuition fees for Scottish students. English students planning to study in Scotland should consult   http://www.saas.gov.uk/student_support/scottish_inside/index.htm for up-to-date information.
3 You may not be able to register initially for a degree in psychology because there is often a filter controlling entry to later years of the more popular degree courses, following a more general course involving several other academic disciplines to begin with.

Research

As well as teaching undergraduates, many university staff will be spending a significant part of their time running research, often with postgraduate research students and research assistants. This will be partly funded by earmarked funds that the university receives for research, and partly by outside funds from industry and the research councils. Departments with a very strong research emphasis, particularly those in the Russell Group, will have a rather different atmosphere from other institutions. Their resources, particularly for experimental work, may be better and their teaching will perhaps be nearer the cutting edge of the discipline. However, their teaching will probably be less intense and more dependent on the input from postgraduate students in supervising practicals and tutorials, and they may expect more in the way of independent learning from

---

[1] They are also different in Wales and the Republic of Ireland.

their undergraduate students. This is an important factor to take into account both when choosing a university and in the way you plan your learning after you have arrived.

What to do if things go wrong

The first rule here is to take action sooner rather than later if you are getting into difficulties.

Try to help yourself by reading the course documents and asking your fellow students. Failing that – ask! There are several places where you could seek help: the learning resource centre will have subject librarians, many lecture courses have associated chat rooms, most departments have a secretary or administrator who knows everything, or at least knows where to find it, or you could email the lecturer if the problem relates to a specific course.

If you cannot solve the problem, tell your tutor in particular, that you are in trouble. It is much easier for them to organize help early on than if you wait until you have missed the deadline on a coursework assignment, or failed a part of the course. If you have a personal crisis that constitutes 'mitigating circumstances', it may be possible to arrange an extension; if you do not understand something, they can help you to sort it out. But they cannot do the work for you.

If you feel you have been hard done by, it may be possible to make a formal appeal. This cannot be made on the basis of academic judgement, but any kind of procedural error, wrong information or anything that makes you feel you have not been fairly treated is a legitimate basis for an appeal. The students' union will help you here and advise you on how to go about it.

The students' union will also help if the complaint lies the other way and you are subject to a disciplinary hearing – often providing someone to attend the hearing with you, explain things and give you advice. Universities are fairly tolerant places, however, and if you keep an eye on the limited number of rules, you are unlikely to come to grief.

2

Organizing inputs

Learning begins with collecting information on a topic, understanding it, recording it for future reference, and then organizing and mastering it to make cogent arguments. This chapter discusses the opportunities for gathering information available to you in a university, and the strategies you might use to exploit these effectively.

2.1 What kind of student are you?

Individual learning styles

One sensible place to start is with yourself. You are after all studying psychology! John Flavell coined the term **metacognition** to describe the ability to reflect on one's own thinking processes (Flavell, 1979). So, what do you know about yourself and how you like to tackle things? For example, one of us has a very strong visual memory and can always remember the exact whereabouts of something on a page – even if we cannot remember what it says!

Think what has worked for you in the past – are you an early bird or a night owl? Or neither! Will it be more effective to plan work for assignments at

particular times of the day? If you are in paid employment during your course your options may be limited and you need to plan carefully to make the most effective use of your precious time for studying. Each hour of formal teaching will require several hours of your own time to prepare and follow up afterwards. Psychology, as you might expect, has something to say about this. Pask (1988), for example, divided learners into serialists and holists. Serialists are concerned with mastering the material a step at a time, whereas holists like to get a feel for the overall thinking on the topic before they get down to the detail. Josephs and Smithers (1975) make a somewhat different distinction between 'syllabus bound' styles of learning, where things are tackled in a logical sequence, and 'syllabus free', where the learner plays around more freely with ideas. These represent the extremes of a whole range of preferred learning styles and recognizing where you fit will help you to tackle things to best effect. Of course, different styles will be appropriate in different situations. For example, practical work demands a more syllabus-bound and serialist approach, **psychoanalysis** a more syllabus-free and holistic one.

Another important difference between people is in the way they find it most efficient to learn new material – for example, in their ability to learn by rote. At the extremes, some people with **autism** find rote learning extraordinarily easy, while it is very hard for people with certain kinds of **dyslexia** (Blakemore & Frith, 2005). Most of us fall between these extremes and we need to develop learning strategies that match our abilities.

Some people find **mnemonics** valuable in helping them learn otherwise not very meaningful material, particularly lists (Harris & Morris, 1984). **Acronyms** that spell a word from the initials of a list, like OCEAN for the components of the **Big Five** (see Appendix 4) are the simplest example. Making up a sentence from the initials is another way. We remember the order of the colours of a rainbow – red, orange, yellow, green, blue, indigo, violet – by the mnemonic 'Richard Of York Gave Battle In Vain'. The sillier it is, the more memorable it is likely to be, but it does need to make some kind of sense because it is the meaning that makes the mnemonic memorable. Another system, for people who have strong visual imagery, is to imagine placing the words or objects to be remembered around a familiar location (Maguire, Valentine, Wilding & Kapur, 2003). Although these techniques are probably not very helpful unless you want to impress your friends by memorizing chunks of the telephone directory, they might be worth a try for arbitrary lists of things.

If the institution offers a student mentor or 'buddy' from the second or third year, do not be too proud to accept and to ask them how they tackle organizing their work. They will probably be able to tell you things to avoid as well as things to do, and they can also brief you on any short cuts or on the things in all institutions that can safely be ignored without incurring official rebuff.

Active learning

Try to develop a more active learning style. If you do not understand what I mean, try the following exercise.

Exercise 2.1 An experiment in active learning

Ask someone to take you on quite a complicated, unfamiliar route, ideally driving you in a car or taxi, and then try to retrace it later. Compare this to a situation where you have had to find your own way, perhaps using a map or directions, and then try to repeat it. You will be astonished at the difference in your success in the two conditions.

The distinction between active and passive learning styles dates from the work of Eric Fromm (1979). In a passive learning condition, the student listens to lectures, takes notes, memorizes and reproduces the material for the required assessments without really reflecting upon it, whereas during active learning the student becomes much more involved in the material being presented, critically evaluating it, thinking through the implications, noting questions and issues, and trying to relate it to other observations or information of their own. Although some people are more easily disposed in terms of their personality to be active or passive learners, active learning skills can be developed by adopting this particular mindset, and engaging with ideas and information on the course and reflecting upon them, leading to improvements in understanding and critical appreciation. It is notable that some students paddle along in passive mode until the impending examinations galvanize them into trying to really get to grips with their subject, and only at this point do they begin to appreciate quite how interesting it is.

Tips: Putting things in your own words

➤ There is good evidence that you are much more likely to remember material that you have organized yourself and put into your own words, however roughly, which is why study groups and seminars are such effective ways of learning.
➤ As E.M. Forster (1976, p. 99) said, "How do I know what I think until I see what I say?"
➤ This is also a good way of checking that you have understood everything and that you have identified the further work that needs to be done.

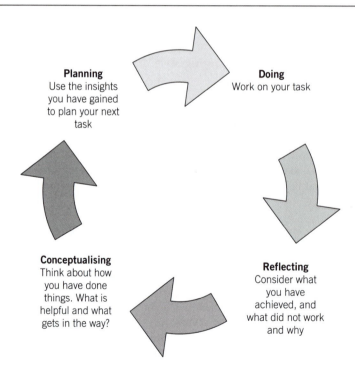

Planning
Use the insights you have gained to plan your next task

Doing
Work on your task

Conceptualising
Think about how you have done things. What is helpful and what gets in the way?

Reflecting
Consider what you have achieved, and what did not work and why

Figure 2.1. Kolb's model of a reflective learning cycle.

Kolb (1984), in rather similar vein, developed a model of effective experiential learning and the reflective learning cycle (see Figure 2.1).

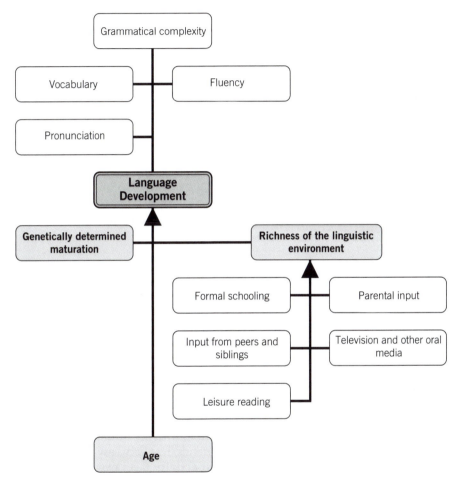

Figure 2.2. An example of a tree diagram used to organize the material on a topic, in this case the factors affecting the development of language.

You are also much more likely to retain information if you have somewhere to 'hang' it in your mind. One technique is to set up a mental tree and populate the branches with anything you think you already understand about the topic, amending it and adding new information as you go along. Start by jotting down everything you can think of on a particular topic in a random fashion and then try to organize it in logical ways. (See Figure 2.2)

Exercise 2.2 Developing an active learning style

Try asking yourself the following questions before you engage with a new topic, to build a more active learning style.

- What do I already know about this?
- Have I had any experiences of relevance to the topic?
- Have I got any ideas, however basic, from reading articles or watching TV programmes on the subject?
- Where is the author coming from? Are they viewing the topic from a particular theoretical standpoint?
- Is the evidence the author gives reliable and valid?
- Where is the author going? What is their conclusion going to be?
- Are there possible alternative conclusions the author has ignored?
- What implications could this have?

Managing your time effectively

Your university schedule will not look like a school timetable, although there will be regular weekly scheduled events such as lectures and practicals. However, some things will happen less often. You may have fortnightly tutorials, for example, or occasional meetings with your tutor, or with other students if you are involved in a group project. Keep a diary – whether it is on paper or electronic does not matter but you must be able to access it constantly. This is also invaluable for planning your work and your social life.

By this stage in your career, you will have realized that people prefer to do some things rather than others, and tend to do them first. Given the many possibilities that will be open to you in your new institution, whether through the students' union, the psychology department or new friends, it is very easy for studying to drop to the bottom priority as **displacement activity** takes over. You can learn to manage yourself very well once you understand this. Vacuuming the stairs is almost our least favourite occupation but when we lived in a two-storey house, it was very difficult to get on with the PhD because it was always just less preferable, but when we moved to one with four storeys, writing the thesis became infinitely preferable to cleaning three flights of stairs!

> ## Tips: Making effective use of your time
>
> ➤ Monitoring progress helps you make progress:
>
>   ○ make a list with achievable goals
>   ○ keep it with you
>   ○ put reminders on your mobile leading up to key dates
>   ○ cross things off as you do them.
>
> ➤ Rewarding progress helps you make progress:
>
>   ○ give yourself rewards from time to time – small rewards for small advances; large rewards for large advances (see '**operant conditioning**' in the Glossary, Appendix 4)
>   ○ space these out so that you always have something to look forward to.

There is good experimental evidence that learning is most efficient when arousal is at an optimal level, and tails off when someone is over- or under-aroused (Yerkes & Dodson, 1908). This is illustrated by the **inverted U-shaped curve** in Figure 2.3.

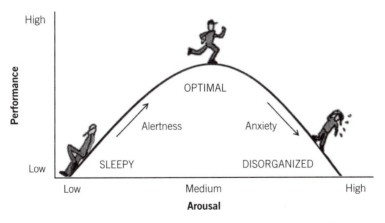

Figure 2.3. An inverted U-shaped curve illustrating the Yerkes–Dodson Law.

2.2 Structuring information

Original work in psychology tends to be reported in three main ways that, to some extent, reflect the life cycle of new research and ideas.

First, there is the conference, which tends to be where new research is first given an airing and 'test driven' among a peer group of researchers for comment and criticism.

Conference material is normally published only in the form of abstracts, either in journals or on the web, and is often in too preliminary a form to use as a reference.

Then, most new research, particularly in the more scientific branches of psychology, will be presented in a **paper** to a psychological **journal**. There is a large and growing number of journals within different areas of psychology and there is a certain pecking order in terms of reputation. If a discovery is of major interest or importance it may make it into a prestigious general journal such as *Nature* or *Science*. If it is quite specialized it may appear in one of the top refereed journals in that area. A refereed journal is one that sends out all the papers offered to other researchers in that area and asks them to comment, a process known as **peer review**. Recent research in an area is likely to be found here. A very useful source for finding recent articles on a particular subject is Psychological Abstracts, which pulls together abstracts from the main psychology journals, enabling you to monitor new developments. It is available as a CD-ROM known as PsychLIT. **PsychINFO**, which is now available at most universities, offers a web-based search of Psychological Abstracts.

Finally, the research may find its way into books, either a reflective piece by the researcher, drawing together a range of his/her experimental work in an area, or in a book or review article by someone else, surveying the current state of knowledge in a particular area. (See the section on 'Collecting additional material', page 95, for more detail on this.)

Planning

Like all activities, whether climbing a mountain, going on holiday or cooking a meal, studying psychology will benefit from some forward planning. This will help you both to get to grips effectively with the course and make it more enjoyable. Too many students, particularly at the beginning of their course, wander around in the forest without a map, unable to see the wood for the trees, gathering up information without knowing quite how to handle it. This is sometimes called the Christopher Columbus phenomenon because, when he set out, he did not know where he was going, when he was there he did not know where he was, and when he returned he did not know where he had been.

A degree course is very different from A-level or other level 3 qualifications in that you will be expected to take responsibility for yourself and your learning. There are considerable sources of help at your disposal, however – and we say more about these in the section on 'References and finding your own sources', below (page 35) – but they cannot do the work for you. Teaching in higher education tries to put the student at the centre of the experience and, considerably aided by IT, the lecturer becomes 'not a sage on the stage, but a guide by your side'. However, lecturers vary in their approach to university teaching, so be prepared for both sage and guide teaching models.

Filing

Good filing is the key to coping well with the course, and you will probably end up with both paper and electronic filing systems as information will arrive in different formats from different sources. Decide how you are going to tackle your filing and try to keep it up to date. Even rapidly scanning something in order to file it correctly is a way of rehearsing it, which will help you to remember it.

One simple, if old-fashioned, paper-based way is to have different-coloured files for each lecture course or subject area, and use dividers for different topics. Write your notes on ready-punched paper pads and file them as soon as possible. This is one situation where you should not skimp on paper – having to tear a sheet in half because the contents need to go in two different places is far from ideal!

After a week or two of trial and error you may well decide that your filing system is not ideal for coping with all the material coming in, so review it and change it right away – not in the middle of your last year.

Some people find it helpful to have the main points on any topic summarized on index cards, which can be recombined for different situations such as writing an essay or preparing answers when revising. You might find it helpful to do this as you go along as part of your active learning strategy, and better than just passively skimming through your notes after a lecture.

Some lecturers very helpfully give out copies of PowerPoint slides with space for you to make your own notes alongside theirs, even if you have to print the notes off for yourself from the course website. Find out if this is the case and make a point of running them off before the lecture so you can annotate them yourself during the lecture – part of your active learning stance. When reading around the subject you can then interleave your own notes so they are all in the same place when you need them for an essay or to revise.

Inevitably, some of your material will be on the web and easier to incorporate into folders and files on a computer. This has the advantage that you can easily move or copy bits of text into other folders where they are also of relevance. Make full use of the organizing structures in the software when setting up your folders so that you have a hierarchy of information (see Figure 2.4) and can find things very quickly by following the branching substructure, rather than having to hunt through lots of files all at the same level. As things develop, some good house-keeping will pay dividends. Get into the habit of pressing the 'save' button as you write, and back up your files regularly to protect against more major computer

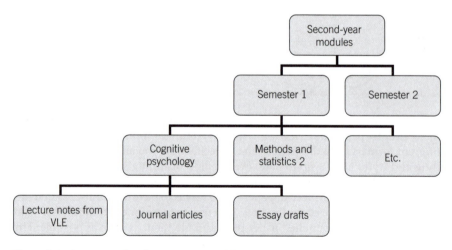

Figure 2.4. An example of an electronic filing system.

disasters (there is more on this on page 82). If you are working up an essay, date each draft as you save it and clear folders of earlier drafts. Having to open several versions of something to work out which is the current one is a pain, as we know to our cost in writing this book!

It pays to be very strict with yourself about filing things properly right from the start using clear and systematic file names. There is nothing worse than trawling through badly labelled files hunting for something. If you have not got an appropriate folder set up, stop and make one (and label it) there and then. It may not seem important during the first half of the first term – in fact it may seem like bureaucratic overload – but material will quickly start to pile up and, if you have designed your system to cope, it will avoid having to go back and fiddle with it later on.

Discover how to use Google Desktop, it is a godsend when you just cannot locate something. It functions just like Google on the web, but on your own material: it can search your own files, and work you have stored on your hard drive, and it can also set up an index.

Tips: Filing

➢ Filing is not a substitute for learning. Try to make sure that:

- you understand everything (or almost everything) before you file it
- your notes are clear enough to be comprehensible when you start to revise for an exam
- the logic to your filing system is clear so you will be able to find things again some time later (achieving this is part of the active learning process)
- the material is filed in the correct place.

➢ Avoid filing things unread if you can possibly help it.

Notes on notes

Effective note taking should not just be a mechanistic process of recording information, and you will find you cannot do this in lectures in any case as they run too fast. Rather, concentrate on making brief, clear summaries with key names and terms that you can use like a map later on. If you are busy writing down the lecturer's jokes (should you be fortunate enough to stumble across one with a sense of humour) you will miss the key concepts that are being introduced and the theories that are being explored.

TOMtip

❖ Try right from the start to imagine yourself coming back to this information as you begin to revise for an exam, and think how it will be helpful to have it organized

There are some simple techniques that will enable you to cope when there is much you want to record. If you already have a shorthand system of your own, skip this bit, otherwise a few minutes thinking about how to develop a system that will enable you to take things down faster and more economically will pay huge dividends. One obvious technique is to develop abbreviations and signs, particularly for words you will come across repeatedly, such as 'psychology', and use them consistently. Some of those in common usage are given in Figure 2.5.

ψ	psychology
S	subject
P	participant
Expt	experiment
&	and
>	greater than
<	less than
∴	therefore
∵	because
=	equals
≠	is different from
←	before
→	after
⇒	resulting in
∧	above
∨	below
q.v.	quod vide = which see *or* see also
ibid	see the same reference
e.g.	for example
i.e.	in other words

Figure 2.5. Useful symbols and abbreviations to use when taking notes.

You can also abbreviate word endings, as shown below.

testing	$test^g$
simulation	$simulat^n$

And you can use all the usual texting abbreviations, but you must remember not to use them in your formal written work. Many technical or anatomical terms have standard abbreviations (see Appendix 3) such as LGN for lateral geniculate nucleus. However, always be careful to spell out names and dates in full and clearly, because you will need these as pegs on which to hang the rest.

Rather than trying to take things down in traditional note form – in sections with headings – you might find it more useful to catch the content in a diagram. Take the different approaches to psychiatry, for example, which could be summarized in a similar way to that shown in Figure 2.6.

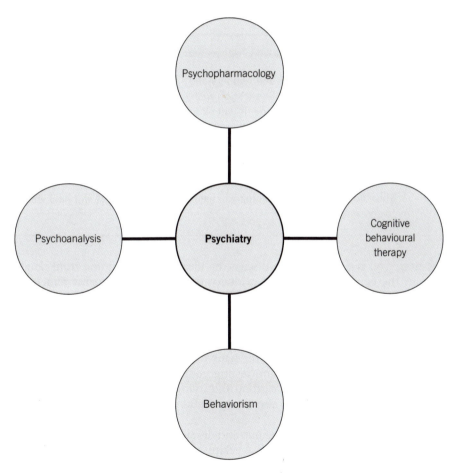

Figure 2.6. An example of a radial diagram showing some different approaches to psychiatry.

This is a particularly good technique for annotating a seminar and it will leave you with a useful map of the ground covered (although you may want to re-draw it afterwards). A good seminar chair will spend the last few minutes pulling together the discussion and summarizing the main points covered. If this does not happen you should try to do it for yourself. It is easy to miss things if you do not organize your thoughts properly. Remember to leave spaces around and between your notes so that you can add additional points, perhaps in a different colour, as you come across them.

Tip: Annotating notes

➤   Develop a convention for annotating anything you read. For example:

  ?   for something you don't understand
  R   (**references**) any reference you wish to follow up
  !   to mark a particular point that strikes you as significant
  E   (essay) anything of immediate relevance to your current assign-
      ment
  D   (dictionary) any terms you need to look up
  __ underscore new names or terms.

This simple method of keeping you listening in active mode will help you to concentrate.

The more you can rehearse and discuss the ideas and information from taught sessions the better. There is good evidence that university students remember material much better if they have regularly attempted to summarize and explain facts and theories in their own words (Butler & Roediger, 2007; McDaniel, Anderson, Derbish, & Morrisette, 2007). These studies were done by setting students regular short-answer tests. If your modules provide these, then make the most of them. If they do not, then get into the habit of identifying a list of the topics you have covered in the last week and testing yourself on describing them. Either way, it will pay off. Working in a group and trying to describe something so that someone else understands it is also a very useful way of discovering if you have grasped it yourself.

Even going for a coffee or to the pub and discussing the lecture or seminar with your friends is a very good way of checking your understanding, and will help you to be more confident when you get into a seminar or start on an essay. Failing this you could use the chat room (see page 70) on the course website to explore your understanding with others or check any points.

> ### Tip: Keeping files by you
>
> ➤ · When you have filed your notes, do not stick the file away until an assessment deadline looms, keep them in sight, and relate new information and ideas back to them.

References and finding your own sources

The best references to follow up are usually the ones the lecturer gives. They should be the most up-to-date sources and will have been chosen for their appropriateness and relevance. They should certainly be where you start your own reading.

However, as your expertise develops you will want to put your own slant on things, or you may be writing on a topic of your own choosing for which you have not been given any reading. In either case, you will want to do a literature search to find your own sources. There are now extremely powerful electronic databases for doing this, which are discussed in more detail in Chapter 3 (page 73). Trawling round the web, especially at the beginning of the course, may well waste a great deal of time and not be very helpful. Material on the web is not always edited unless it is on a reputable website, such as that of another university, and even then could be **biased**, inaccurate or out of date. One useful exception is the *Intute* discipline-based website set up especially for students (see page 81). It is better to concentrate on finding journal articles rather than pieces written just for the web. However, misleading conclusions can appear even in journals and, as you understand more about potential methodological weaknesses, you will become better able to identify these. Simply faking data unfortunately also happens, such as some of the nature/nurture work on twins done by Sir Cyril Burt in the first half of the twentieth century and which were very influential in developing education policies (Mackintosh, 1995; Tucker, 1997).

> ### Tips: Reliable sources of useful information
>
> ➤ A relevant authoritative source, for example an article by a recognized researcher in an established journal, which will have been through a system of 'peer review' where other researchers working in the area have read the paper on commented on it.
> ➤ Something that is widely cited and well supported by subsequent papers.
> ➤ Something that has been borne out by later **experiments** that replicate the findings.

> ➤ Learned academies, like universities or research institutes, which publish things on their own websites.
> ➤ Articles by the original researcher, or by other researchers following up the work in the original source.

It is quite possible to follow a trail backwards through the literature from a recent article. Look for a recent review, usually identifiable from the title, or failing that a longish article on the topic that might have a useful review in the introduction. The *Annual Review of Psychology* and the *Psychological Bulletin* are both good sources for broad overviews on particular topics.

Another useful strategy, if you have been given a classic article written some time ago as a starting point, is to find recent articles or reviews that cite (refer to) it. Databases such as Web of Knowledge enable you to do this (see the section on Subscribed databases, page 73). You might even be able to help bring your lecturers up to date on a topic on which they are a bit rusty. They will certainly be impressed and might even be grateful.

TOMtip

❖ Lecturers are human too. After reading 57 essays that simply regurgitate their lecture notes and the set texts, a novel finding or viewpoint will create a glowing **halo effect** to influence the mark you get.

Spending money on books

One of the first decisions you will have to make is whether to buy the recommended textbooks, which may add up to a considerable cost over the modules and years of the course. This is a tricky one and depends on a number of factors, which will vary from institution to institution and person to person.

Tips: Buying textbooks

> ➤ Before you rush out to buy a textbook, ask yourself the following questions.
>
> ○ Is the module taught largely from a single book, or does the lecturer give lots of other book and journal references?
> ○ Has the lecturer indicated that the module is examined from a single textbook? (This is mainly likely if the exam is multiple choice, where textbooks often provide a battery of possible questions that

the lecturer will draw from, and is more likely in the first year than later on when you will be expected to have read more widely.)
- How many copies are there in the library, particularly in the reserved access section, and how many students are on the module?
- Will I be working mainly in the library or will I want to have access to books at home?
- Will the book be useful for other modules, perhaps in later years?
- Is this a topic I am particularly interested in?
- Is this a topic I will have difficulty with, and will therefore depend heavily on the textbook to support me?
- Can I save money by buying a second-hand copy from the students' union or bookshop, making sure it is the latest edition?
- Will I be able to get some of my money back by selling the book at the end of the course?
- Could I share books with someone else?
- And, last but not least, how much money do I want to spend in total?

➤ An analysis like this tends to lead to the following best buys:

- a general introductory text that covers the whole subject and will be useful as background reference right through the course
- first-year textbooks, particularly ones with multiple-choice question tests on sections
- statistics and methodology textbooks, particularly ones that will guide you through the statistical software package you will be using right through the course
- books on areas that may lead to a future career.

How to read a book!

It is not usually effective to read psychology books like novels, starting at page one and reading right through to the end. With textbooks it is pretty obvious that you find the relevant chapter (using the outline of contents in the chapter headings at the front) or section (using the index at the back).

This book, for example, is designed to function both like a novel and like a textbook. It would be useful to read it right through at the beginning of your course. However, you can also treat it as a reference book, turning back to particular sections or chapters as they become particularly relevant to what you are doing at that moment. For example, if you are faced with something specific like making a presentation for the first time, look up 'Presentations' in the index, but if you need more general help at a particular stage in the course – for example, tackling a research project in the last year – turn to the chapter labelled 'Research projects and dissertations' on the contents page.

Exercise 2.3 explores this process in a bit more detail. Suppose you were reading round in preparation for writing an essay on the psychology of colour vision and you found R.L. Gregory's book *Eye and Brain* (Gregory, 1998) from your reading list in the library.

Exercise 2.3 Three stages in reading a book for an essay on colour vision

1 Flip through it first. (This flip-through stage seems so important that a friend of ours introduced it into his web-based learning material.)
   • Does it look interesting? *(Yes, and it has plenty of good illustrations – important in a book on vision.)*
   • Does it appear to be at about your level? *(It looks fairly approachable, so should be a good introduction.)*
   • Is it reasonably digestible? *(The odd paragraph tested reads very easily.)*
   • When was it published? (You should normally concentrate on recent material, say less than five years old or still in print, unless you have been specifically referred to a 'classic'.) *(It is still in print even though it was published in 1998.)*
   • Has it run into many editions – a sure indication of its usefulness – and do you have the latest edition? *(It has been continuously in print since 1966 and is now in its fifth revised edition.)*
2 Then consider the content.
   • Has it got an abstract (summary) at the beginning to give you more idea of what it covers? *(No.)*
   • Look at the chapter headings for a more detailed indication of what it covers. *(You will probably decide that Chapters 1–4 are a relevant introduction and definitely worth reading.)*
   • Decide which chapters are particularly relevant to the task in hand. *(Obviously Chapter 7 'Seeing colours').*
   • You could check in the index to see whether there are references to colour in other chapters. *(Yes.)*
3 Finally, run through some checks.
   • You might check whether there are other references to particular things in Chapter 7 elsewhere in the book, e.g. Thomas Young *(no)* or Helmholtz *(yes).*
   • Then check the other chapter headings. *(Chapter 9 'Realities of art' might be just the thing to help you develop a discussion of the implications of how we see colour but in fact it is mainly about representing space.)*
   • Then look for further references you might follow up. *(Helpfully arranged here by chapter at the end.)*

Now you are ready to take some notes (see page 31).

Speed reading journal articles

During the whole length of your psychology course you will be given large numbers of references to articles in scientific journals and, particularly in later years, you will be doing literature searches to find journal articles of your own (see Chapter 3, page 80). The sheer number can be overwhelming, so you need to develop techniques for scanning them quickly. This is not an easy skill to learn so do not be upset if you find it hard to master. There was a recent debate about the necessity of applying speed-reading skills in the context of the Mann-Booker prize where the jury members have to read a large number of novels in rather a short timescale, and this is much easier than reading scientific papers. Luckily nearly all psychology articles are written in a similar format. They usually have six sections: Abstract, Introduction, Methods, Results, Discussion, References. (This is the format you will use yourself for writing up practicals and projects; see Chapter 4, page 113) One standard approach is to read the Abstract, then the first and last paragraph of the Introduction and the first and last paragraph of the Discussion.

Even if your institution does not subscribe to the journal containing the article, associated abstracts can usually be found in online databases (see Chapter 3, page 73). Read the abstract carefully. What you do next depends on how clear you found this and why you are reading the paper. If you just want to cite a specific straightforward or well-established experimental finding or observation and the Abstract is clear, then this may be enough. If you are not certain exactly what is being reported then look at the Methods and Results sections in enough detail to clarify things, and move on. If you are reporting a contentious or **paradigm**-shifting paper, then you will want to be more evaluative. In this case read the Methods and Results sections more carefully to ensure that the findings are valid and support the conclusions being drawn. If the paper is central to the topic you are working on, then you will also want to read the Introduction and Discussion sections fully to get ideas to incorporate into your work or to find other sources to follow up. As with a book, you should rarely sit down and read the paper right through in the order it is printed. The only exception would be if you are presenting a summary of the paper at a seminar.

Tips: Reading journal articles

➢ Authors of journal articles often produce a brief and user-friendly summary of their results and conclusions at the beginning of the Discussion section at the end of the article.
➢ Papers reporting several experiments may have a short Discussion section after each experiment explaining why the next experiment was done, followed by a General Discussion section at the end.

Critical and analytical skills

The key objective in reading is not only to acquire psychological knowledge but also to hone your critical and analytical skills. These are transferable skills that you will take with you when you graduate into whatever field you choose to work in, so it is worth paying it some attention. Critical thinking is not in fact about being critical, it is about being alert and taking nothing for granted. Bensley (2008, p. 128) defines it as "reflective thinking in which a person reasons about relevant evidence to draw a sound or good conclusion". A critical disposition is typified by:

- open-mindedness
- intellectual curiosity
- clear reasoning
- sceptical attitude.

Exercise 2.4 Developing critical skills

- Start by considering the author's starting point of view. Does it originate from some vague common-sense belief? What argument is presented for you to accept this?
- What is the line of reasoning? Does it stand up logically? Does it contain any assertions that are unsupported?
- Can you detect any flaws or hidden assumptions?
- What is the evidence? Identify different kinds of evidence from literature reviews. This may take the form of examples, earlier experiments, surveys or case histories, depending on the nature of the paper. Does it come from a reliable, disinterested source? This is particularly relevant with studies involving drugs, where the source of funding for the work should be identified. The less classy the evidence cited, the more sceptical you should be.
- Does the evidence actually support the argument? Look carefully at the reasoning behind the methodology and the statistical tests used. (The most common mistake here is known as the **'tertium quid'** – in other words, a third hidden factor. The assumption is made that, because two things appear to vary together, one causes the other, whereas they may both be affected by a third factor that has not been identified (see Experiment 1 on page 156).)
- Can you detect any experimenter bias?
- What precisely are the conclusions?
- Can the conclusions really be derived from the evidence? Keep an open mind to unexpected outcomes.
- Are there reputable replications of the findings?

2.3 Formal teaching

The teaching components making up a psychology degree course will vary from module to module, but will normally comprise some of the following four different elements: lectures, seminars, practicals and tutorials.

Lectures

Lectures form the stereotypical experience of universities. Every film about students will have a scene where a lecture hall of rapt students listen entranced to a lecturer unfolding a subject with crystal clarity. Unfortunately, not all lecturers are like Indiana Jones and, particularly as group sizes increase with widening participation, you will need some strategies for survival.

Lectures form the backbone of most psychology courses and you should certainly plan to attend them. They provide an overview and framework for the course, and a guide and introduction to the various topics on the syllabus, giving key concepts and theories. Do not try to write everything down, you can get some of the detail from the recommended textbook afterwards or, better still, before. Handouts from the lecturer are a very useful record and save you having to scribble things down the whole time so that you can think about what is being said and make your own additions.

Getting course notes from a friend or from the web, if they are available, is not an alternative to attending in person. This is not because lecturers get lonely, though they do, but because you will miss out on the finer detail and the comments in parentheses that make the subject come alive. (Actually, we once knew a lecturer, in the days before student evaluations, who we are sure taught in a deliberately incomprehensible way so that the students stopped coming after a couple of lectures and he could get back to his research.)

Tips: Active learning in lectures

➢ Attending a lecture is worthwhile only if you do it actively. (If you are going to doze or chat to your friends, it is fairer to yourself, the other students and the lecturer to do that somewhere else.) So:

   ○ be there on time to hear the lecturer set the scene
   ○ take notes – but organize them, during the lecture or afterwards, in ways that are meaningful to you
   ○ identify areas that will need further work, either because the lecturer skipped over them or because you have not understood what is being said
   ○ add your own thoughts, ideas and queries
   ○ ask questions, either during the lecture if given the opportunity, or afterwards.

There is no need to be shy. Gilovich, Medvec and Savitsky (2000) demonstrated in a fun experiment on what they termed the 'social spotlight' effect, that we tend to overestimate the attention that other people are paying to us. He persuaded students to wear a Barry Manilow T-shirt into a lecture, to their huge embarrassment, and found that they massively overestimated the number of people who noticed.

> **TOMtip**
>
> ❖ If you do not understand something, it is likely that half the people in the room do not understand it either. So it is helpful to everyone if you ask a question about it as it gives the lecturer a chance to clarify, and other students will be grateful.

Seminars

Seminars vary enormously between institutions and between lecturers, but they are generally intended to be an opportunity for rather more active learning than is possible in a lecture. They usually require some output from the students and this is discussed in Chapter 4 in the section entitled 'Contributing to seminars' (page 120).

In general, what you get out of a seminar will be roughly proportionate to what you put in. There is no short cut for skivers! If you turn up not having done the preparation that has been set (usually background reading), you will just be a passive spectator and miss a wonderful opportunity to explore the material. If all the students in your group behave this way, then the seminar is going to be extremely dull and a waste of time. Do debate the arguments and ask questions.

Although they can appear somewhat daunting, don't, whatever you do, just miss the seminar because you have not quite got your act together. On the one hand, attendance registers are sometimes taken, but much more importantly you will be missing one of the major opportunities to sharpen your mind, for which you came to university.

Class practicals

Practical classes complement the more theoretical inputs on a course, giving you the chance to explore some of the basic skills (and problems) involved in doing psychological research. They can vary in nature across the whole spectrum of courses that comprise a degree in psychology, from descriptive behavioural observations to experiments involving equipment and statistical analysis of the results. They should give you a feel for what it is like to do research in psychology, and can be enormous fun. (For more detail on practical work see Chapter 5 'Research projects and dissertations'.)

As always, do not just passively follow the instructions you are given. Consider why it is being suggested you should do something in such a way, or whether there are alternative, perhaps even better, methods that could be used. Thoughts like this will be useful material when you come to write the report on what you did.

> ## Tip: Sampling research seminars
>
> ➢ Many departments have research seminars when staff or visiting speakers talk about their research. Students are usually very welcome at these and they offer an excellent way of getting a feel for how real research works, what sorts of issues come up, and how difficult it can be. If you are lucky, you may get a chance to see and hear someone that you have heard about in lectures or read about in books.

Inevitably some of the practical work will involve statistical analysis (see also page 154) and the statistics teaching you receive may reflect either of two different approaches. Some lecturers believe that in order to use a statistical test you must understand properly how it works; others favour much more of a 'cookbook' approach. So the first task is to decide which of the two is appropriate for your data. People are not naturally good at handling probability and a good example of this is the 'gambler's fallacy', which feeds the profits of casinos worldwide and is based quite simply on the feeling that, after a run of bad luck, things must change. Try this for yourself by taking a coin and asking a friend predict the outcome on each throw. After a run of tails, most people will tend to believe that heads is more likely to come up, whereas the probability (0.5) remains exactly the same on every throw.

Experimental design and statistics

These will loom large right from the start. Most degree programmes include experimental design and statistics lectures at both level 1 and level 2, and few final-year research projects are complete without a statistical analysis. There is a psychological reason why psychology needs statistics and Daniel Kahneman won the Nobel Prize in 2002 for helping elucidate it. Quite simply, people are lousy at judging evidence without the help of statistics.

Kahneman showed in one of the classic papers in psychology (Kahneman & Tversky, 1973) that, in making judgements and predictions, we ignore relevant evidence, are influenced by irrelevant evidence, and are generally overconfident about the validity of our decisions even, and this is the frightening bit, when we know that the evidence on which it is based is unreliable. This is not just about numbers, although this is an important part of it. One particular number that people are very bad at taking into account is the base rate against which data are collected, a phenomenon sometimes known as **base rate neglect**. If we see more broken-down Fords than Jaguars, we tend to assume that Fords are less reliable, ignoring the fact that there are many times more Fords driving round than Jaguars.

Exercise 2.5 Neglecting base rates

Try for yourself this real-life problem, which was given to health professionals, whose day-to-day job involves just this kind of decision, and pregnant women, who might be faced with it too (from Bramwell, West & Salmon, 2006).

The serum test screens pregnant women for babies with Down's syndrome.

The test is a very good one, but not perfect.

Roughly 1% of babies have Down's syndrome.

If the baby has Down's syndrome, there is a 90% chance that the result of the serum test will be positive.

If the baby is unaffected, there is still a 1% chance that the result will be positive.

A pregnant woman has been tested and the result is positive.

What is the chance that her baby actually has Down's syndrome?

Now turn to Appendix 2 to find out what the right answer is and how to calculate it. The answers of the health professionals are also there. If you got the answer wrong, you will see that you are in good company.

Experimental design and statistics are about taking valid decisions about what is true and false, particularly when the evidence is numerical. For example, one of Kahneman's targets from his early days in the Israeli army was the interview. All the evidence suggests that interviews are, for most purposes, a hopeless way of selecting students, which is why most psychology departments gave up using them many years ago. However, even if we know this, we still feel confident in our judgements when we do interview people. We are also particularly bad at intuitive decisions based on numbers and we are, more generally, bad at evaluating decisions when we have made them. So if we are trying to decide whether one psychotherapy is better than another, whether a particular drug affects a particular kind of behaviour, or whether houses with burglar alarms are more or less likely to be burgled, we need careful design and statistics to help us find the truth.

This skill is essential in psychology, but of course, decisions like this pervade our everyday life as well. We are regularly taking decisions about what phone or car to buy, or what to do to keep healthy and slim. So learning how evidence should be collected (the design bit) and evaluated (this is where we may need statistics) to get at the truth and judge whether the advice you are being given is valid or not will be an important skill for you to carry with you for the rest of your life.

Despite their obvious importance most of us approach experimental design and statistics with considerable apprehension. Coming to terms with design, which is about avoiding your data being influenced by factors that you are not interested in or that prevent you measuring what you want to measure, is the easier bit. It involves random assignment to groups, **counterbalancing** testing order to avoid practice effects, and so forth. Identifying confounding variables like these is largely just intelligent common sense. Avoiding them is a bit more difficult, but there are well-developed procedures that you will be introduced to in your methods classes and in any methods textbook.

Statistics are intellectually more challenging. You should not be too worried, though. Andy Field, the author of our favourite, and much praised, statistics textbook writes, "I have a sticky history with maths because I used to be terrible at it. At 13, I was almost bottom of my class, yet 12 years later I'd written a statistics textbook" (Field, 2005, p. xxi).

A second reason why you should not be too worried is that this is another area where base rate neglect rears its ugly head. We fail to take the base rate into account adequately when comparing our own abilities with those of others. In a review of the literature, Dunning, Heath, and Suls (2004, p. 69) conclude that "on average, people say that they are 'above average' in skill (a conclusion that defies statistical probability)". Over-rating one's driving ability is a particularly strong example of this tendency (see, for example, Horswill, Waylen & Tofield (2004). However, and this is the bit that is relevant to coping with statistics, recent work (Moore, 2007) suggests that this illusory self-aggrandisement is limited to common behaviours and abilities. For rarer and less common skills, the tendency is to *underestimate* our abilities. Statistics falls into this category, explaining why people often lack confidence in approaching the subject.

Like cooking, experimental design and statistics can be tackled at two levels. You can do things from first principles, getting to grips with the underlying logic and maths, or in the case of cooking, the properties of different ingredients or flavours. Or you can buy a cookbook and follow the recipe. Think of Andy Field, or whoever wrote your recommended textbook, as the Jamie Oliver of statistics. They are good cooks and you trust their advice enough just to follow the recipe without worrying too much about why you soak some dried pulses before cooking and cook others before soaking them. You just do it and it works. Of course, it is more fun if you understand the underlying principles, and it enables you to cope with novel or tricky situations without disaster – but it really is not essential. In any case, as with cooking, the underlying principles will gradually become easier to understand with practice. It is good to be like Jamie Oliver in the kitchen, launching yourself in with vigour and learning from your mistakes, but, to begin with at least, follow the recipe carefully.

The trickiest bit is to find the right recipe for your particular set of ingredients, or in this case your experimental design. Most textbooks will have some kind of flow diagram (like the example in Figure 2.7) leading you from your particular design to the right recipe (statistical test).

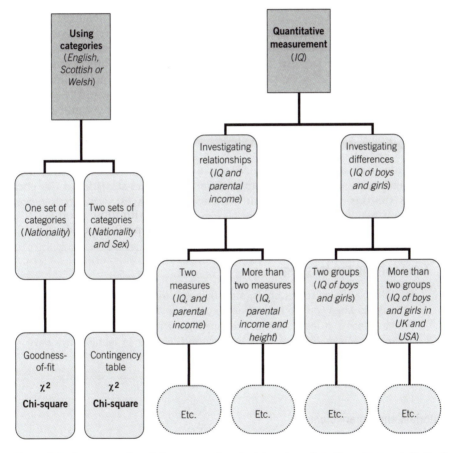

Figure 2.7. An example of the start of a decision tree for choosing a statistical test (examples are given in brackets); the right-hand side would continue with questions until a specific technique or statistical test was indicated.

Tip: Decision tree for choosing statistical tests

➤ When you get your statistics textbook, find the decision tree for choosing a statistical test, bookmark it with a Post-it note, and keep referring to it as you learn about different tests so that you will know how to use it when you come to analyse your own data.

Having decided how you are going to analyse your data, but not before, you must now worship at the feet of the great goddess the **Statistical Package for the Social Sciences (SPSS)**. And worship you must – do not put it off. Once she is on your side she will be invaluable for running statistical tests and producing figures (though Excel can also help here, see the section on 'Site licensed software', page 72). Take full advantage of all the teaching you get on SPSS and spend time working through some examples in your recommended text. Learn particularly how to enter data into her spreadsheet. It can be a cause of great frustration and time-wasting when, for example, at the end of your final-year research project you spend a day entering months of carefully collected data into SPSS, only to discover that you have put it in the wrong way round and have to do it all again. That said, SPSS is a wonderful weapon in the battle against ignorance. By enabling us to perform **inferential statistics** at the click of a few buttons, she validates our evidence and gets us a few steps nearer the truth.

Tip: Learning the language

➤ Like psychologists, or chefs, statisticians have a language of their own. Just as when you are holidaying abroad, you will feel a bit lost until you have learnt at least some of the language. The language is precise, but may vary slightly from book to book and lecturer to lecturer. We have defined some of the more common terms in Appendix 5.

Tutorials and supervisions

Tutorials and supervision sessions usually involve a smaller group than seminars, and are based on individual discussion, possibly triggered by something you have written, a problem you have identified or something you have been asked to read. In some universities they are formally timetabled in a small group, in others the student makes an appointment or just turns up to see their tutor during tutorial hours, which are published either for the individual tutor or as standard tutorial slots across the whole psychology department timetable.

As with seminars, the value you get out of them is largely dependent on how much you put into them. Go prepared with questions or with problems you are having with your work. The other students in the group will probably have similar issues and you may be able to share ideas on how to resolve them. Make use of your particular tutor's expertise, try looking them up on the web or on the university website to find out their research specialism and what other departmental roles they hold apart from teaching. If they are a postgraduate student, find out from them what they are working on.

Tutorials also offer a good opportunity to raise general questions about the course or the university system. Even if your tutor does not know the answer, they may know someone who does on the former, or the right branch of the central administration to approach on the latter (see the section on 'Central services' in Chapter 1, page 15).

2.4 Learning in groups

Many psychology courses have elements where it is a requirement to work formally in teams, and much can be gained by working informally in study groups. Both methods offer excellent preparation for employment, where it is almost certain that you will have to work as part of a team and interpersonal skills are much in demand.

Contexts where group working may be required include seminars, projects, practicals and placements.

Issues to consider

Group working on the course can add hugely to the enjoyment of your work but it does create a few issues that need thinking through.

- Working together requires timetabling and planning. Failure to turn up or deliver on time wastes everyone else's time. Efficient use of email can vastly facilitate group arrangements.
- Considerable time will be required to pull individual contributions together for a joint project or assignment and you must allow for this. Deciding early on how outputs are to be presented and agreeing a common format will save time and angst.

- If there are more than two people, it is probably efficient to have a chair, although different elements of the task can – and should – be delegated to particular members, but consider carefully what personal attributes will make the best chair.
- Distinguish between the roles of leader and chair. Some tasks, usually those requiring fairly quick decisions and action, benefit from a leader, especially if this person possesses superior knowledge or prior experience. An example might be going on an expedition where people must act together to achieve the goal without debating every step. (We have all been on trips where more time is spent debating the interpretation of the map than actually walking!) More reflective tasks, which should draw on the knowledge and expertise across the group, will be more productive with a chair who can hold the ring, drawing in contributions from everybody and structuring the discussion to make best use of everybody's input.
- Poor group dynamics can spoil any project and some thought should be given to this. Laying out the conventions for how the group will operate is a good first step to avoid trouble, and takes less time than trying to mend a group that has fallen out!
- It can be difficult to give formal recognition for the individual contribution that members have made to a project, particularly if this is one that contributes marks for a degree.
- How to deal with 'freeloaders' or disruptive team members is something that you may need to learn – it is a skill that is likely to be highly useful in the future.
- Groups composed of people with very different attributes are particularly good at problem solving in changing situations, so try to put together a group from different backgrounds.
- Contrary to general belief it has been found (e.g. Nijstad, Stroebe, & Lodewijkx, 2006) that people working individually produce a wider range of solutions than when working as a group, although they tend to enjoy the group working more. So it can be a useful strategy to agree to split up to think about ideas, then meet again after a day or two to pool what you have come up with.

Advantages of group working

Some of the advantages of group working include:

- covering more ground
- giving access to a wider range of expertise
- mutual support
- seeing how other people learn

- making friends
- motivation
- having fun.

But note that this does not include letting someone else do all the hard work!

Figure 2.8. The Mad Hatter's Tea Party from *Alice's Adventures in Wonderland* by Lewis Carroll (1865), illustrated by John Tenniel: a perfect example of a dysfunctional group.

TOMtip

❖ Remember that everyone else will have anxieties about group work too, but will show them in different ways.

Assessing your own interpersonal skills

As a psychologist (and as a person) it might be useful to think about your own interpersonal skills. You could even get someone else to rate them and incorporate the outcome into your personal development profile (see Figure 2.9).

	Poor	Medium	Good	Excellent
Listening to others and responding				
Facilitating others by eye contact, nodding				
Making own points effectively				
Team-building skills				
Intervening to preserve balance of power				
Leadership skills				

Figure 2.9. Checklist for evaluating interpersonal skills in a group setting.

Another way of learning more about your strengths and weaknesses in a group situation is through a **simulation**. Simulations are very useful in psychology because, by setting a very precisely defined task that everybody comes to on equal terms without differential prior knowledge, we can control some of the variables that confuse real-life situations, enabling us to look at the factors we are interested in more clearly. They give **participants** the opportunity to receive feedback on how they have behaved, examine the consequences and consider how to improve.

Exercise 2.6 Observing group behaviour

See if you can find a group working on something together and ask if you can observe. You could use the simple observation sheet in Figure 2.9, or one we have developed from an original constructed by Bales (1958), which captures actual examples of behaviour (Figure 2.10). Do not participate in the discussion. Write the names of participants along the top and place a tick in the matrix every time you see one of them showing the behaviours listed. Try to record specific events rather than a general impression. This will emerge at the end.

Look at the collection of ticks for different participants in each of the three sections. You will easily be able to identify the leader(s) (mainly a), the productive team members (mainly b) and the saboteurs (considerable c). People may change their roles as the agenda progresses.

Names of participants	——	——	——	——	——	——	——
(a) Task-orientated behaviour							
Offers new ideas							
Explains things to others							
Reminds others what has been said							
Builds on others' ideas							
Asks for information							
(b) Group-supporting behaviour							
Agrees with others							
Tries to get consensus							
Tries to stop arguments							
Encourages others' ideas							
Concern for hygiene factors – opens window, makes coffee, etc.							
(c) Negative behaviour							
Challenges others' authority							
Knocks others' ideas							
Actively disengaged – yawns, looks out of window							
Tries to take over							
Distracts group from task							

Figure 2.10. Observation sheet (after Bales, 1958).

2.5 Learning through experience

Work experience

The three useful outcomes of work experience are:

1 evidence of generic 'employability' (i.e. you turn up on time, get on with other people and deliver to deadlines)
2 evidence of commitment to a particular area of work, particularly in caring and educational areas
3 and, obviously, income.

Relevant work experience will increase the insights you obtain from your degree course and play a significant part in obtaining entry to some of the more competitive postgraduate training programmes, such as clinical psychology. You will probably have to undertake more work experience than that provided by a placement during your degree, so it is worth putting in some time and effort to get the most benefit from any work you undertake.
Work experience falls into three main types, as described below.

1) Types of work experience you may encounter as part of your course

- *Work-based project:* a specific piece of assessed work for your course, usually undertaken at an employer's premises, which is common in the third year.
- *Work placement:* many psychology courses include opportunities for placements with a range of employers who take on psychology graduates. Look out for a list, if there is one, and sign up early. More commonly, you will have to work hard to find a placement on your own, so start early and be prepared to make lots of contacts before you find one that will accept you. It will be well worth it, not least because it will enable you demonstrate some work experience in job applications later on, and will give you insights into the issues that arise when trying to move from theory to application. It is particularly important if you want to go into one of the practising applied branches of psychology, such as clinical, where experience is an important factor in getting on to highly competitive training courses. Remember to make best use of the career development and student employment services that your university offers when thinking of finding a relevant placement (see our associated website (www.openup.co.uk./psychologysuccess)) for details of relevant work experience for entering different branches of psychology).
- *Sandwich year:* a one-year period of assessed, and usually paid, work that forms part of your degree, usually during the third year of a four-year course. These

are quite rare in psychology courses and, at the time of writing, are offered by only nine universities, sometimes associated with joint degrees involving ICT or human resource management.

The 'Prospects' website (see www.work-experience.org) asked people who work in the field for a definition of quality work experience, and the following list is what they came up with:

- the student is trained by the higher education institution (HEI) to identify potential learning outcomes
- objectives are set (by HEI, employer and student)
- supervision is by a supervisor trained in the objectives and learning outcomes of work experience – academic supervision and visits take place
- regular feedback is given
- an appraisal is given during the work experience and at the end
- where appropriate, a project is undertaken
- learning and achievements are articulated by the student in written form
- an assessment is made, including an assessment of the skills developed (by HEI, employer and student)
- recognition – credit or a certificate is awarded.

2) Different kinds of paid employment you can fix up for yourself

(Check with your university careers service whether there is a local specialist agency to help with this. In Liverpool, a universities-based agency called Business Bridge negotiates with regional employers to find part-time and temporary work that is relevant to the student's degree subject; this project is so successful that many students take up full-time employment with them when they graduate.)

- *Part-time work:* during term-time, but be realistic about the amount of time and energy you will need for your course, and leave some time to relax.
- *Vacation work:* the summer is a good time to find this, often filling in while other staff take family holidays. A temping agency might take you on as a regular for vacation work.
- *Internship:* a term increasingly used by large companies, referring to a placement, usually during the summer vacation.
- *Shell Step:* vacation work experience for full-time second-year undergraduate students only, where they undertake a specific project within a small to medium-sized business during an eight-week placement in the summer vacation (see www.shellstep.org.uk). They are paid a weekly training allowance, which is exempt from tax and national insurance. Shell Step offers

an induction session, mid-term review, and training in report writing and presentation skills. Participants are eligible for awards at local, regional, and national levels.

3) Unpaid forms of work experience

- *Voluntary work:* any type of work undertaken for no payment, usually in your spare time.

(For a scheme that provides assessment and accreditation of part-time and voluntary work, particularly for school leavers, look at details of the CRAC Insight Plus programme on www.insightplus.co.uk.)

- *Work shadowing:* where a student observes a member of staff working in an organization, and so gains an understanding of what a particular job entails.

Tips: First thoughts on careers

> ➤ Think about likely career interests and the skills you want to develop.
> ➤ Use placements to gain a greater understanding of the career choices open to psychology graduates, whether within psychology or in another sector.
> ➤ Consider how much time you can spare while you are studying.
> ➤ Identify relevant employers with the help of your University Careers Service and research them using the **internet**.
> ➤ State clearly what you can offer them in terms of skills from your course, other activities and personal qualities.
> ➤ Successful work experience could make a significant difference to your career, so treat it professionally.

Some frequently asked questions:

Is work experience really required?
If you are applying for certain postgraduate courses in psychology, it is essential. In any case so many people have degrees these days that anything that makes you look different when applying for jobs is helpful. Employers increasingly want evidence that recent graduates can fit in straight away.

Can I leave this until later?
Use your time at university to get a range of experiences so that you have some idea what you want to do when you graduate. In your final year you will be concentrating on your exams and project work.

Is one form of work experience more valuable than another?

Postgraduate admissions tutors in psychology know that it is often difficult to come by assistant psychologist posts or other recommended forms of experience. However, you can develop the required skills through part-time or voluntary work using the PDP formats on page 59 to articulate your achievements to admissions tutors and potential employers.

What if I'm just making the tea?

Ask for a review of the agreement. Taking students on for work experience or even temporary work requires that someone organizes where you fit in, and sometimes you just have to smile and volunteer until they get used to you. If you get nowhere – leave.

What about payment?

Get this clear before you start. If the placement is part of your course (except, in our experience, sandwich years) or if it is voluntary work, you cannot expect to be paid. Otherwise the employer is legally obliged to pay you. Your students' union will have information about the current minimum wage. However, you know what the post is worth to you (and how short of cash you are).

Experiment participation schemes

Many departments, particularly those very active in research, ask first-year students to act as participants in research studies being run by staff, postgraduates, or level 3 students. This will be called something like the Experiment Participation Scheme (EPS) or the Experiment Participation Requirement (EPR), and you will gain credit of some kind for completing it. It has two important functions. It supports the department's research activity, something you too will appreciate when you run a research project in your final year. More importantly, it will give you the opportunity to find out what kind of research projects are being done in your department, to experience for yourself some of the methodologies that will be talked about in lectures, and a feel for what it is like to be a participant in a psychological experiment. All these will prove very valuable when you come to plan your own research project, so it is worth taking the exercise seriously, thinking about what the experimenter is doing and talking to them afterwards about their experimental design.

2.6 Personal development profiling

(Also known as PDR (personal development review) or PPP (personal profiling and planning.)

You may already have had some experience of this with Progress Files at school. Personal development profiling (PDP) is defined by the Quality Assurance Agency for Higher Education (commonly known as QAA) as: "a structured and supported process undertaken by an individual to reflect upon their own learning, performance and/or achievement and to plan for their personal, educational and career development". (2000, para. 11).

This sounds a bit of a mouthful, but the process can be very helpful in drawing out what you have learned while you are doing your degree, particularly when you are considering what course options to take, what to do next after your degree, and when you come to fill in application forms for further qualifications or employment. It will also help you to develop reflective skills, and understand better what motivates you and where your hang-ups lie. Your department may have adopted a formal process for personal development tutorials with your tutor, using specific web-based software, but if not you can tackle it on your own. The three key processes are:

1 reviewing everything you do
2 reflecting on it
3 planning what should come next.

This is a very good way of monitoring your progress as it brings together the formal record of your achievement for your course, experiences you have had during practicals/ placements, particular thoughts you may have on either of these, and things you have done during your leisure or part-time work. If you are a mature student, this record of lifelong learning will be particularly helpful in viewing your degree in the context of all your other experience and understanding more about yourself, as it brings individual personal reflection alongside the more objective record from your course as complementary parts of the learning process.

Skills gained during a degree in psychology

The QAA assesses and monitors the quality of all higher education provision and, in conjunction with all the higher education institutions offering degrees in psychology, it produced the statement, shown in Figure 2.11, of the typical skills a graduate in psychology should expect to acquire. You could refer to it from time to time as a useful checklist of your progress.

If you refer to the statement of intended learning outcomes associated with each module of your course, you can see where the formal course will reckon to cover these, and where you may need to take things into your own hands to augment the standard degree provision.

Subject specific skills

On graduating with an honours degree in psychology, students should typically be able to:

- reason scientifically, understand the role of evidence and make critical judgements about arguments in psychology
- adopt multiple perspectives and systematically analyse the relationships between them
- detect meaningful patterns in behaviour and experience and evaluate their significance
- pose, operationalise and critique research questions
- demonstrate substantial competence in research skills through practical activities
- reason statistically and use a range of statistical methods with confidence
- competently initiate, design, conduct and report an empirically-based research project under appropriate supervision, and recognise its theoretical, practical and methodological implications and limitations
- be aware of ethical principles and approval procedures and demonstrate these in relation to personal study, particularly with regard to the research project, and be aware of the ethical context of psychology as a discipline.

Generic skills

On graduating with an honours degree in psychology, students should typically be able to:

- communicate ideas and research findings, both effectively and fluently, by written, oral and visual means
- comprehend and use numerical, statistical and other forms of data, particularly in the context of presenting and analysing complex data sets
- be computer literate and confident in using word processing, database and statistical software
- solve problems by clarifying questions, considering alternative solutions and evaluating outcomes
- be sensitive to, and react appropriately to, contextual and interpersonal factors in groups and teams
- undertake self-directed study and project management, in order to meet desired objectives
- take charge of their own learning, and reflect and evaluate personal strengths and weaknesses for the purposes of future learning.

Source: Quality Assurance Agency for Higher Education, 2007, pp. 10–11

Figure 2.11. Extract from *The Subject Benchmark Statement for Psychology.*

Stages in the personal development profiling (PDP) process

In order to be an effective learner it is useful to be able to articulate to yourself (and others) what you know and what you do not know. As Donald Rumsfeld said in a rather different context:

> There are known knowns; there are things we know we know. We also know there are known unknowns; that is to say we know there are some things we do not know. But there are also unknown unknowns – the ones we don't know we don't know. (US Department of Defense Briefing, 12th February 2002)

The PDP process is a bit like running a **SWOT analysis** (Strengths, Weaknesses, Opportunities, Threats) over yourself from time to time, and one very encouraging outcome is that it reminds you of the progress you have made since the last time.

The introduction of PDP in British universities followed Lord Dearing's Report on Higher Education (HMSO, 1997), in which he concluded that students would benefit from structured support to become more aware of themselves and how to learn, how to improve their personal performance and, most particularly, to help them with the transition from university to their chosen career. It turns the concept of a degree from a relatively passive experience, where you sign up for and complete the various elements on your course in a prescribed manner, to one in which you are in the driving seat and take charge of all aspects of your university life. In other words, this supports active learning at its best. The process should help you to be more confident and enjoy your degree course more, and is an ideal preparation for lifelong learning, both in your career and in your personal life.

PDP consists of three parts:

1 the PDP process
2 a personal record of goals, achievements and plans
3 a transcript that sits alongside your degree certificate and gives more information about your achievements, what you have studied and any work experience you have had.

PDP can seem rather a laborious process but it can be significantly lightened by the use of appropriate software, which will do half the job for you by offering prompts and formats for your progress file. One of our universities uses a web-based PDP support tool called LUSID, which is quite popular in universities in the north-west, but there are many other versions, and you should check whether your department uses one and how to access it. The key function should be to enable you to send your preparation to your tutor in the standard format, store your records and use them to produce a CV. The crucial point to realize is that no one has access to this personal development record but you. Your tutor sees only the elements you email to them.

Try limbering up by doing the following exercise. The results may surprise you. We have spent a great deal of time on platforms at degree-awarding ceremonies feeling sorry for students who have obtained only 2.2s or 3rds, but noticing that they did not seem particularly upset about it. Then the penny began to drop. They were just pleased to have obtained a degree and had set their future aspirations accordingly. A degree class does not brand you for ever (see page 164) and, once in employment, what you achieved yesterday rather than several years ago at university comes increasingly into play.

Exercise 2.7 What do I hope to gain from my psychology course?

	Essential	Desirable
Obtain a degree Obtain a 2.1, which will enable me to continue PG studies in psychology A passport into a career in psychology Gain a better understanding of psychology Have more insight into my own and others' behaviour Intellectual challenge Meet interesting people Make congenial friends Experience student lifestyle Get a well-paid job Get a fulfilling job Take part in student politics Experience different working contexts through placements Gain confidence Develop a range of skills Problem-solving ability Experiment with new things		

There is a wide variety of PDP schemes which are merely a formal system for structuring the relationship between student and tutor and how far the scheme is used will depend very much on the tutor's attitude and the conventions in the department.

A typical PDP programme set out with your tutor may run something like that shown in Table 2.1. The key point is to identify the things you particularly need to work on and set target dates for completion, but make them realistic.

The tutor's role is not so much to comment upon the feedback you are receiving but to support and help you while you construct a plan of action arising from them. By the time you get to the end of the course, you will have the elements of a full CV – with all details captured in the right place – on which to draw.

Table 2.1
A typical PDP programme
First semester

Beginning	**Task** Write a statement saying why you chose this course and what you expect to gain from it
	This first tutorial is really an opportunity to get to know your tutor, ask them any questions you may have and raise any concerns
Middle	**Task** Write a statement summarizing your initial impressions of the course
	This is the moment to consider any feedback you have received and check any areas of uncertainty with your tutor
End	**Task** Collate and summarize any feedback you have received so far on assignments, identifying your own strengths and weaknesses
	Plan proposed actions in discussion with your tutor as a result

Second semester

End	**Task** Review all the feedback from work so far
	Start to identify areas you are good at and areas where you need some further development; statistics is often an area that students coming from arts backgrounds find difficult, for example; find out what help is available and set some timescales

Third semester

End	**Task** Review all assessment outcomes so far
	Consider whether there are gaps in your experience that you would like to fill to help you to think more about your future career direction; can these be met though optional module choices or placements with particular employers? This is the time to experiment with different aspects of psychology; deciding what you do not want to do is helpful in narrowing the range of possibilities, and you may get surprises.

3

Using IT

The effective use of information technology (IT) will help you at all stages of your course so it is vital that you understand what it can do for you. Like psychology itself, it is a fast-moving world, so you should keep checking throughout the time you are studying that you have kept up to date. However, an understanding of the content of this chapter will provide a sound foundation onto which new developments can be built.

3.1 Using learning resource centres

All universities and colleges used to have libraries. Nowadays many of them have learning resource centres (LRCs) instead. They are the same thing. However, the change of name indicates an important shift of emphasis. While they used to store just hard copies of books and **journals**, now they are also, and perhaps more importantly, gateways to the global world of electronic data processing and digital information.

To use this cornucopia you will need to have a proof of identity, usually your university student card, and a username and password for electronic access. So step one is to make sure these are all in order. This will give you access not only to your own university's library but to all other university libraries as well. Although your borrowing rights will be more limited in other universities, they can be a valuable resource, particularly if you happen to be near one in vacation periods.

The ways in which universities manage their learning resources differ. In some cases, particularly in smaller institutions, the library and computing facilities will be run as a single operation, and there will be single help desks and web pages. In others they will be managed separately, and there may be separate helpdesks and web pages. Listen to the briefings at the start of term to find out how your institutions resources are organized.

Accessing books and journals

Books are a form of information technology and remain indispensable. University libraries can be rather intimidating places, with several storeys of book-shelves (usually known as stacks in large libraries) on a daunting range of topics. It is therefore essential that you make an effort as soon as possible to begin to familiarize yourself with the layout so that you become comfortable about wandering round its nooks and crannies without feeling you are an intruder. It is *your* library and the sooner you feel comfortable in it, the sooner you will start making effective use of its resources. Go to any induction sessions or guided tours that are laid on for you. There is so much to take in, particularly in the first weeks, that you probably will not remember it all, but make a note of things to follow up, identify the place to go for help and do not be afraid to ask for it. Librarians have two jobs: keeping the place in good order and helping users find the information they want. A good librarian gets pleasure from both, even if the demands of the two roles sometimes conflict!

If your induction session offers exercises, it is very tempting to skip these and go off for a coffee. Don't. This is a good example of the benefits of active learning and if you have already used the catalogue and tracked down a few books and web addresses while there is support available, you will find you have remembered what to do when you come to tackle your first assignment some weeks later.

Tip: Explore thoroughly

➤ Explore your library/learning resource centre thoroughly in the first few weeks. Identify where the psychology books and journals are, and make a note of the best places to work.

➤ Keep exploring. A good library is always changing and when you come back for a new academic year you may find a different layout or useful new facilities.

There are two ways of finding your way round a large library and you should use both. The most important is the catalogue. You can access this from any computer terminal and usually nowadays from any computer linked to the web. If you know the author or title of a book, you can use this information to find where it is kept. However, most catalogues are much more powerful than this. You can use them for searching by topic, subject or keyword.

Exercise 3.1 Using a library catalogue

To find out how useful your library catalogue is, log on to it to see if it will enable you to search by keyword/topic. If it does, try entering the following terms:

- crowd psychology
- statistics
- **theory of mind**
- visual cortex
- **autism**
- face recognition
- eating behaviour.

In each case you will probably find sources with varying degrees of relevance and usefulness. Try to pick out one or two that would be useful starting points for finding information or writing an essay on the topic. Checking the date of publication and the location is helpful here. If the book is in the philosophy section, it will probably not be as useful as if it is in the psychology section.

Now make a note of the catalogue number of one of these books and, next time you are in the library, go to this part of the stacks and see if there are any other useful books nearby on the same topic.

The other way to find a book on a particular topic is to go to the section on the stacks where books on this topic are grouped. Until you are very familiar with the library, you will probably need to start by finding this section in the catalogue. Remember, too, that cataloguing is a subjective business and you may find two books on the same topic in different sections. When you have found the section, look for recent books on the topic or books with multiple copies, indicating that at some point they have been recommended on a reading list, but check when they were published – they may be on the shelves rather than being read because they are out of date.

There will be several different kinds of material stored in your library. The two main ones in the psychology section will be books and journals. Journals come out, like magazines, at regular intervals and are eventually bound in volumes or grouped in boxes to put on the stacks. So there will be current issues of journals in one place and bound or boxed volumes of back issues on the stacks. There may also be offprints, which are copies of individual articles from journals, or book chapters that lecturers have identified as being particularly useful. There will probably be a collection of videos and films, and there may be some psychological tests, though these will probably be available only to authorized people. PhD and Master's theses written by the university's postgraduate students will also be kept in the library, and even sometimes undergraduate dissertations, which can be useful exemplars when you come to write up your own project or dissertation in your final year.

Different kinds of material will be stored in different places and will have different loan arrangements. These will vary from university to university, in particular the length of time you may keep borrowed books. Typically, there will be three kinds of use permitted.

1 *Material that can only be used in the library:* this will include recent issues of journals, reference books such as dictionaries or encyclopaedias, and particularly valuable books. These will not normally be kept on the standard shelves, although most of them will be on open access so you can go and take them off the shelves yourself. Some of them, particularly the valuable books, will be in a closed access section, so you have to ask a librarian to fetch them out for you.
2 *Material that is in high demand and can be borrowed for only a short time (for example, a few hours or overnight):* lecturers will ask for multiple copies of set texts and important offprints of journal articles to be put in this section. These may also be on closed access shelves but, like everything in the library, they will be listed in the catalogue.
3 *Books and back copies of journals on open access shelves, which can be borrowed for longer periods:* there will usually be some copies of set texts in this category, but you will have to get in early to find them.

Another useful resource your library will give you access to is the inter-library loan facility. If you cannot find the book or journal you are looking for in your library, you can ask for it to be borrowed, or photocopied if it is a journal article, from another library. This can be quite expensive, and libraries will usually ask for a contribution to the cost. Most inter-library loans are obtained from the British Library, and you will be able to access its catalogue, as well as many other library catalogues, through your library's home page.

University libraries are very sensitive to student needs. If you have problems let them know, either by speaking directly to the librarian who is responsible for your subject area, or through your student representatives. You will also be able to recommend the purchase of new books. Your recommendations will always be considered but resources may not always be available to meet them. It will also probably take a little while for the purchasing and cataloguing to be done to make them available, but there are usually procedures for accelerating these if, for example, a lecturer suddenly recommends a new 'essential' textbook.

TOMtip

❖   Your library or learning resource centre is only as good as the feedback it receives. If there are problems, tell the staff. One thing is certain, nothing will be done about a problem if the librarians do not know about it. They may not be able to do anything about the problem quickly, but at least those who follow on from you will be grateful.

Accessing IT

In various places in your learning resource centre, and scattered around the university too, you will find clusters of computers (almost always PCs) for students to use on a first-come-first-served basis. There will also probably be Wi-Fi access so that you can use your own laptop if you prefer. In either case, to log on, you will need your university username and password.

The university's computers will be set up to give quick and easy access to a range of in-house electronic resources (see the section on 'Using in-house electronic resources', which starts on page 69) and will be very useful even if you own your own laptop.

When you log on to a university computer with your username and password for the first time, you will see the standard university screen desktop with much of this software already installed and accessible through icons on the desktop. When you open the web browser provided, you will find it has been set up so that the home page is the university **portal**. This will give you quick access to the web-based resources and information on the university's **intranet**, such as its virtual learning environment (VLE) (see page 69) and the library catalogue. The portal displays a content page for many of the electronic resources that the university provides and, though you could make something else your web home page if you wanted to, you will benefit from keeping it as the portal. You will want to change other things, like adding icons to the desktop and saving favourites and links to the web browser. When you log out, these will be saved as your personal profile on the university's central computer, or server. Next time you log on to any university machine, your own personal settings will appear again.

If you are doing your own work on a university computer, you will be able to store information in two ways.

1 You will be allocated some space on a central university memory store. If you

look in My Computer or Windows Explorer you will find the normal C:drive, which is the memory on the computer you are working on. However, there will also be some other drives. Some of these will be for the university's use only, but there will be one that you can use to store your files. At Liverpool University, among others, this is labelled the M:drive (for me or memory?), which is a nice **mnemonic**, but it could have any arbitrary label. So check in an induction session, or in the introductory leaflets on computing that you will have been given, or at the help desk, what it is called at your university. The important thing is that files on this drive will be backed up every night and will therefore be very secure. You use it just like the C:drive and you will normally be able to access it off-campus (see page 78).

2   Alternatively you will be able to plug in your own portable storage, memory stick or CD, onto which you can save material. This will be more flexible but less secure. Most people use a mixture of the two.

One thing you should not do is to try to save work directly on to the desktop or C:drive on the university machine you are working on – this will risk losing it altogether.

University computers will give you easy access to the printers that will be strategically placed among the sets of computers. Although you will probably have to pay something towards printing, the cost will be heavily subsidized. There will also be printers available for doing more elaborate work in colour or on larger-sized paper – for posters, for example – but these are likely to be centrally placed.

Tips: Getting the best from your LRC

➤   Consider using the LRC at less popular times. They tend to be very quiet first thing in the morning!

➤   At busy times of the year – for example, near the end of term when lots of coursework has to be handed in – there may be electronic queues for university printers. If you are relying on these printers for your own work, build in one or two days' slack in case of problems. (This is a wise thing to do even if you use your own printer, because problems can always arise there too, and 'printer problems' are not an acceptable excuse for late submission.)

The university will have a number of ways of helping you find your way around its IT provision. As well as the leaflets and briefings you will be given when you arrive, there will be strategically placed help desks, which you can visit personally, contact by email (try helpdesk@youruniversity.ac.uk) or telephone.

Tip: Monitoring a changing world

➤   Keep an eye on the guidance leaflets and websites for computing to look out for new resources. This is particularly important at the start of later years of your course because new hardware and software is often added over the summer.

3.2 Using in-house electronic resources

The university will provide you with access to a wide range of often very expensive electronic resources. We list a few of the obvious ones here, but explore the desktop on your university's computers thoroughly, and the websites and leaflets provided, to find out what is available.

The virtual learning environment (VLE)

The university's virtual learning environment (VLE) will be the centre of your academic universe. These are sometimes known as learning platforms, which is a good description of their function. They provide a platform of information onto which you build your own independent study. They are a good starting point, but remember that to get to the finishing post you will need to do a great deal of work outside the VLE, particularly in later years. The most common VLE used in universities is Blackboard, but even if this has been adopted it is often given a local name specific to a particular university.

Different universities use their VLEs in different ways and to a different extent, and so, more strikingly, do different lecturers within an institution. However, the framework is usually the same. Each module for which you are registered will have its own section. Some departments may also have a general section that all their students can access, where they put handbooks and other general information (if not they may put this material on a separate department web page), but the central feature of the VLE is the module sections. Typically, each of these module sections has the ability to provide the following:

- general information about the module, its structure and its assessment
- announcements about changes to the module, etc.
- information about and contact details for the staff teaching the module
- a place for lecturers to put their PowerPoint slides or other teaching material
- a place to put additional teaching material, videos, offprints, etc.
- links to other useful websites
- discussion boards (chat rooms) for staff and students
- assessments, particularly multiple-choice tests and exercises
- a gateway for the electronic submission of essays and other coursework, and the screening of these for **collusion** and plagiarism (see pages 84–90)
- student evaluation questionnaires for you to provide feedback on the module.

The first four of these are the most widely used by staff (and also by students). If your lecturers are not using them, encourage them to do so. Keep an eye on the other parts, though, in case something useful appears halfway through the module.

You will find that some lecturers put their PowerPoint slides or other teaching material on the VLE before the lecture, and expect you to have looked at it and probably printed it off before the lecture (see page 30). Others will say they want you to concentrate on what they are saying, making your own notes in the lecture, and will only make the slides available afterwards. Check to see what is expected for each module.

Tip: VLE access

➤   If you are unable to access the section of your VLE for a particular module, it almost certainly means you are not officially registered for that module. Check.

University email and personal web pages

Almost as important as the VLE, when you register the university will provide you with an email address. It is essential you use this. Your tutor, the department and the university will send round-robin instructions to this address and ignorance is no excuse. So even if you want to continue using your existing address, you must get into the habit of checking both.

Tip: Joining up email addresses

➤ It is annoying to monitor two email addresses, so arrange to forward mail from your personal email to your university email address.

If you are using Microsoft Outlook for running your personal email, go to:

'Tools' (on main menu bar)
'Rules and alerts'
'New rules'
'Start from a blank rule'
'Check messages when they arrive'
'Next'

You can then select any particular conditions you want to use. For example, to forward mail to your university email tick:

'Where my name is in the To or Cc box'
'Next'
'Forward it to *people or distribution list*'

Click 'people or distribution list' and put in your name with your university email address from your contacts list. Then click:

'Next'
'Finish'

Another reason for using the university's email system is that it will give you access to an address book giving the email address and department for all students, useful socially, and addresses and telephone numbers of staff. There will be a number of ways you can access your university email, but the simplest way is usually through a Webmail link on your university portal.

You may also be provided with some personal web space for you to use if you are familiar with setting up web pages, but this is will almost certainly be limited to the university's intranet and will not be visible outside it. One increasing use of this facility in psychology is for running web-based **experiments** and question-naires as part of final-year projects (see pages 139–140).

Site licensed software

The university will have purchased the licences to put a wide range of software on all its networked computers and some of this software will be available to put on your own computer. If it is available to download from the university's intranet, this may be free. Some will simply cost the price of the media, usually CDs. Some you will have to buy through a dealer, but usually at a negotiated rate much cheaper than you could get elsewhere.

A typical range of site-licensed software would include the following.

- The *Microsoft Office* suite, of which the three most important to you will be:
  - *Word*, for word processing, simple drawing, flow diagrams, tables, etc.
  - *Excel*, for creating spreadsheets of data, drawing graphs and doing some basic statistical analysis
  - *PowerPoint*, for preparing slides for presentations and preparing figures for putting in Word, etc.
- **SPSS (Statistical Package for the Social Sciences)**, for doing more sophis-ticated statistical analysis and for drawing graphs and tables.
- *Adobe Acrobat*, for reading and editing pdf files, the format in which journals and books are most commonly stored electronically.
- *PaintShop Pro* or *PhotoShop*, for editing photographs and other pictures.
- Software for drawing, like *Corel Draw*.
- **Bibliographic software**, like *Endnote* or *Reference Manager*, for storing and organizing **references** to books and journal articles, and for automatically placing these in what you are writing.
- Software for sending and organizing emails, like *Outlook*.
- Virus protection software, like *Sophos* or *McAfee*.
- A web browser, such as *Internet Explorer*.

Tips: Using software

➢ If you have a laptop that you use on the web it should have virus detection software installed. If not, the university may be able to sell you a suitable package very cheaply or even provide it free. (It is in the university's inter-est as well as yours that you are protected.) Get it and install it now.

➢ Look out for courses run by the university or your department on the soft-ware packages that you may use. Even if you are reasonably familiar with them, a course often throws up new and better ways of doing things.

> ➤ Training for the **European Computer Driving Licence (ECDL)** is offered by many universities. (There is more information on this in Appendix 4.) This has a modular, self-paced syllabus covering most general areas that you will need. It has the great advantage of giving you an accredited qualification that you can put on your CV.
> ➤ And do not forget that most software packages now have extremely powerful online help facilities.

Subscribed databases

Psychology is a young subject, but it already has an enormous body of evidence on which to draw. The best way into a new topic is usually your lecturer's suggested reading, but sometimes you will be tackling a subject without any guidance and you will also want to go beyond the set reading, particularly for longer dissertations and theses. For this you need a starting point. To find one, the invaluable tools are the electronic databases. These enable you to search almost everything that has ever been written in journals to find, with practice and skill (and a little bit of luck), exactly what you are looking for. Their one weakness is that they are not so good at identifying books or monographs on a topic. Library catalogues, and to some extent Google Books, can help but, as with Google Scholar (see below) they have their limitations.

There are many different databases. The one that is most easily accessible, and free, is of course the open access part of the web. Search engines like Google, with its filtering search engine Google Scholar, which limits the hits to academic sources, allow you to find relevant material. However, there are two big problems with Googling. First, it is totally indiscriminate in its sources, so what you find may be rubbish or, even if brilliant, may be frustratingly unavailable. It is no good identifying the perfect source if you cannot then get hold of it. Full original texts are gradually becoming more accessible and, if they are available, Google is good at finding them. However, publishers work hard at protecting their copyright and the full text is often available on subscription only (see below).

There are two very useful databases for psychologists that get round many of these problems, and that are available if your institution subscribes to them.

1 **PsycINFO**: this is produced by the American Psychological Association (APA), which has been collating abstracts of articles in the majority of psychology journals published in all languages, currently going back to 1806. Where there is no published abstract, it writes it own. Because of this and the inclusion of early work, it is particularly good for historical research.

2 ISI's **Web of Knowledge (WoK)**: this is a commercial database covering a much wider range of disciplines than PsycINFO, so it includes every journal you are

likely to want. It has two main subdivisions. The most useful is *Web of Science*, which, despite its name, covers all academic disciplines. It is probably best to go straight into this to start your search. It began in 1960, and its coverage currently only goes back to the 1940s. A slight weakness is that it relies on the abstracts in the original source and, if these are not present, the only guide to the contents is the title. The other subdivision is *Proceedings*, which covers conference proceedings. Since in psychology these are usually published in journals, it does not normally add much. However, the most recent version of WoK, introduced in October 2007, allows you to do a full search of both together, so the distinction is gradually becoming less important.

The evidence these will provide you with is much more reliable than the web as a whole because they concentrate on **peer-reviewed** journals. Neither is particularly comprehensive in its coverage of books, though this is improving. As you move away from relying on textbooks, journals will be your main source of evidence and these two databases are the place to start hunting it down. Their different strengths mean that it is often a good idea to look in both.

Databases have *fields*. Since PsycINFO and Web of Knowledge were originally established for storing information about journal articles, these are structured towards journals. There are fields for topic, author, article title, date of publication, publication title and, in the case of PsycINFO, many more – it currently has 70 different fields. There are two ways of searching them: the 'Quick' and the 'Advanced'. The quick is simply to put one word in and search all fields, or one particular field. The advanced way is to do what is called a **Boolean search**. This is a pompous name for looking in more than one field at once using a little bit of simple logic by applying the operators AND, OR and NOT.

Exercise 3.2 Finding references

You have been asked to write an essay on the **mere exposure** effect in face perception, but you have not been given any references.

Open up PsycINFO or Web of Knowledge and search the topic field (WoK) or keyword field (PsycINFO) for 'mere exposure'. Note the number of results you get.

Now do the same for 'face', again noting the number of results.

Now combine the two and search for 'mere exposure AND face'. Note the number of results and explore a few by clicking on them to see if they are useful. (If you want to impress your friends, you have just done a Boolean search.)

Now do the same for the other database.

Which database do you think would have been more useful in this case?

As you will have discovered from doing this exercise, the trick of searching databases is to get the outcome down to a manageable number of relevant results.

This may take several goes so, particularly in the early days, always try different ways of searching. It is also well worthwhile exploring the tools that each database provides for doing searches. You will find they differ and it is not until you have played around with them that you discover all the things they can do for you, so try to search, at least the first or second time, when you are not in a rush to find something.

Electronic journals and books

One of the big advantages of the databases Web of Knowledge and PsycINFO is that they can be linked to your university library catalogue to tell you whether a particular reference is available electronically. If it is, you will be able to reach the full article with a couple of mouse clicks, usually from your own machine anywhere in the world as well as from the university computers. The usefulness of this facility will depend on the number of electronic journals to which the library subscribes. Current issues of all journals are now available electronically, but they are often expensive so your library may not subscribe to them. Nor will there usually be electronic versions of early issues of the journals, although these are steadily being scanned in, so it is always worth checking. You will therefore still sometimes have to use the hard copies in your library. The library catalogue will tell you if there is an electronic subscription available and what years it covers. However, you do now often have the choice of reading an article online or in the library. It will be for you to work out your preferred pattern of working, but the speed, flexibility and convenience of working with electronic journals is now very attractive.

Normally you would not bother to save an electronic journal article in your own electronic filing system unless you thought you were going to be referring to it many times, perhaps because it is a valuable review of a central topic in a module or is the basis of a final-year project. If you can afford it, of course, you can also print them out so that you have your own hard copy to carry around, scribble on and read in bed.

Electronic books are not yet as widely available as journals, and the technology for reading on a screen, while fine for journal articles, is arguably not well enough developed for browsing through a long book. You will also need some specialist software – such as ebrary Reader – on the computer you are using, but these are usually available to download free. Unless you have a very big screen for a split display, or several networked computers around you, you cannot have several books open around you online while you are writing on-screen. They do, however, have one big advantage over hard copies and that is the speed with which they can be searched. So if you find that your library does stock an electronic copy of a book in which you want to look something up (and, as always, the catalogue will tell you), then it is very convenient. At the time of writing, not many relevant electronic textbooks are available for psychology, but this is a fast-moving area and most university libraries are rapidly expanding their stock. Our prediction is that by the time the second edition of this book is published, they will have become a much more dominant medium.

Tip: Using 'Favourites'

➤ Put the sites you use most often in your 'Favourites' folder, and the ones you use very often in the 'Links' folder of 'Favourites' so that they appear on the tool bar across the top of your web pages. What you put here depends on your particular style of working, but here are some of the most popular options that often appear on psychology students' tool bars:

- ○ your **internet** bank account (if you have one)
- ○ VLE
- ○ library catalogue
- ○ PsycINFO
- ○ WoK.

What should you buy?

All the resources we have been describing so far will be available to you via the university's computers. Much of the teaching on using these resources will be done on them and it is essential that you familiarize yourself with how they are set up. There will be staff available to advise you how to use them and at least some of them should be available 24 hours a day, so it is perfectly possible to rely on university resources and flourish, especially if you live near the university and do not mind getting up early to find a good place to work. There will also be long periods between lectures when it may be much more convenient to go in and work on a machine in the library or learning resource centre than lug your own laptop around, and, most importantly, the university's back-up system will be totally safe from fire, theft and spilt coffee.

Nevertheless, there is no doubt that having your own IT equipment means you will, while it is working at least, be in control of your own life, and this is something that most of us find attractive. As with deciding what textbooks to buy (page 36), in the end this is a decision you will have to make for yourself. You will have to take into account the following questions.

- How have you been used to working and how do you see yourself working in the future?
- Do you find working in a communal environment motivating or distracting?

- How far from the university will you be living?
- Will you be living somewhere that is networked? (Purpose-built student accommodation will usually be networked nowadays.)
- And, of course, how much can you afford?

If you do decide to set yourself up with independent IT – and, in our experience, nearly everyone does – what should you buy? This is getting into a more technical level of advice and things go out of date very quickly, but here are some guidelines.

- Much as we admire Apple, universities have universally adopted PCs as their standard general-purpose machines. So if you want to be compatible with these, you should adopt one too. (You may still get a chance to use Apple Macs for running experiments in the department.)
- If you are living away from home buy a laptop, but get a reasonably large and high-quality screen. You will be spending long hours in front of it, perhaps working on spreadsheets of numbers, and eyes do get tired.
- If you find the laptop pad annoying, you could buy a mouse to plug into it.
- If you find the keyboard on your laptop fiddly – although people do seem to get used to even the smallest – buy a cheap keyboard to plug into the USB socket.
- It must have networking and Wi-Fi facilities. They all do nowadays, but if you are buying a second-hand one, check.
- The latest operating system and software is nice to have, but not essential. Universities are like oil tankers – slow to change course – so you may find that it takes them a year or two to change to the most recent version of Microsoft Windows.
- It might be worth checking with your university whether it has any financial support or negotiated deals with suppliers to help with the purchase of laptops – not so likely now that prices have dropped so much, but it is always worth asking.
- Our advice would be to buy the equipment before you arrive at university so that you are familiar with it before you start, and are in a position to ask for and take advice on setting it up.
- Microsoft Office, or some other compatible office suite, and a web browser, such as Microsoft's Internet Explorer or Firefox from mozilla.com, are all you will need to begin with. Other software, like SPSS, may become useful later, but you can always add it when you need it.
- You will need a USB memory stick with a reasonable capacity for moving files from your laptop to university machines.
- A reliable printer is a bonus. You can always print in the university, though this will not normally be free.

Tips: Setting up your own computer

➢ If you have not done so already, install Google Desktop. This searches the files on your computer in the same way as Google searches the web – invaluable if you cannot find something. To do this:

  ○ do a Google search for 'google desktop'
  ○ click Google Desktop and download (it offers you some other add-on widgets, which are probably less useful).

➢ If you have any problems in setting up your computer and are not very IT literate yourself, do not worry, there will be plenty of people around at university who will enjoy showing you what you are doing wrong. Do not be afraid to ask: it is a good way of making friends.

Accessing resources from outside and using your own laptop

If you have your own computing equipment it is very important to get it networked if you possibly can. If this is not possible, then you can probably take your laptop into the university and use Wi-Fi to link to the network. If even this is not possible, then you can still use your computer for preparing work but you will

need to use the university's machines for getting your lecturers' notes off the VLE (see pages 69–70) and accessing email. If you are able to network your machine it is worth doing this as quickly as possible. You will start receiving important emails (on your university email address) from the start and you will want to access the university's VLE before the first lecture.

Once you are connected spend some time exploring what you can do (try Exercise 3.3).

Exercise 3.3 Exploring the university intranet

After your laptop is networked and you have your university username and password, open Windows Internet Explorer, or the web browser you are using, and work through the following steps.

1 Find the students' university portal and make this your home page.
2 Find* the university's virtual learning environment (VLE) and add this to the Links bar at the top of your web browser. Or, if you are running Internet Explorer 7 or later and are really keen, you could set up a dedicated tab for the VLE. (If you do not know how to do this, use the Help menu on Explorer.)
3 Find* the university library home page and add this to your Links bar.
4 Explore the library web pages to find where PsycINFO and Web of Knowledge are.
5 Find where you can get advice and information on your university's computing service. (This may be part of the library information or a completely separate set of pages.) Bookmark it.
6 Investigate these web pages to see if the university offers useful software for use on your laptop, either free or cheaply. Examples to look for are anti-virus software and statistical packages such as SPSS (though check with your department that this is used before getting it).
7 Find* the university's webmail page and add this to your Links bar.
8 Go back to the computing information and find the address of the help desk. Add this to your email contacts.
9 If you have problems with any of these, contact the help desk.

* Many of these will already be on the portal and this will probably be the best way to find them initially, but it is still worth adding them to your Links bar so that you have fast access from all other pages.

Your university will almost certainly have set up a system for accessing any files you store on the university 'server'. The accessing routes will vary but find out which route is used by your university from the briefing information on the web pages. You never know, you might be in an internet café in Ibiza and decide you want to consult something you wrote a few weeks earlier!

3.3 Surfing the web and evaluating what you find

We have given this a section on its own because although it is largely common sense, it is really important that you develop your critical skills for distinguishing the wheat from the chaff. All sources on the web should be treated with great caution unless you know who set them up and edits them. There are plenty of nutters out there and psychology attracts its share of them. Web addresses are a good guide and some reliable and valuable resources include those listed below.

- *Websites of other universities and research institutes:*
  - ○ in Britain these have .ac.uk in their web address
  - ○ in the United States and Australia, they have .edu in their address.

  If you have read a **paper** on a topic you are researching, put the author's name and their university into Google and you will usually come up with their web page. Many researchers, keen to have their papers read as widely as possible, will have electronic copies of their papers available through this page, usually as pdf files.
- *Websites set up by researchers* whose papers you have read: so, for example, Simon Baron Cohen who works in the Department of Experimental Psychology at Cambridge University, as well as being Ali G's cousin, has

established the Autism Research Centre. This has its own website (look it up in Google), which is full of valuable articles, reprinted from peer-reviewed journals, and links to other resources on autism.

- *Intute:* this is a free online service set up by UK universities and its address is www.intute.ac.uk. It is created by university subject specialists and provides links to resources on the web with a reasonable degree of quality control. It also has a tutorial aimed specifically at helping psychology students develop their internet research skills (see Exercise 3.4).
- *Psychology Network:* this is a branch of the Higher Education Academy. It is mainly for university staff, but has a developing set of resources for students too, on: http://www.psychology.heacademy.ac.uk/html/students.asp, or Google 'psychology network' and click the 'Students' link.
- *Reference Psyte:* another new site that is being designed to help with writing psychology essays. It gives useful examples of the wrong way to do things as well as the correct way. Its address is: http://www.hud.ac.uk/hhs/dbs/psy/scrips/index.htm, or Google 'reference psyte'.
- *Learned societies:*
  - British Psychological Society
  - American Psychological Society
  - Association for Psychological Science.

  These are probably more useful for careers information, but worth keeping an eye on to see what is going on.
- *Wikipedia:* this can, despite many contrary views, be a useful place to start, giving you explanations, references and links to other sites. Remember, though, that anyone can put information on and they may have an axe to grind or just be plain wrong (there are plenty of examples of the latter). So if you do use it, always check the information by triangulating it with other sources.
- *Bad jokes about psychology:* if you like these and, as you can see, we do, try this site:
  - Psychology Museum at http://www.psych.usyd.edu.au/museum. It also has serious stuff too.
- *Googling:* last but not least, there are the amazing resources given us by our Googlemasters, not just Google itself, but Google Scholar (though see page 73), Google Images for finding figures for your coursework and, probably by the time you read this, Google Essays for downloading completed coursework (but see the section on plagiarism on pages 84–90).

Exercise 3.4 *Intute* tutorial on searching the web for psychology resources

Find the *Internet Psychologist* page on the *Intute* website. It is at: http://www.vts.intute.ac.uk/he/tutorial/psychologist.

Or, more simply, just put 'internet psychologist' into Google and it will come up near the top of the list – along with some people claiming to be clinical psychologists!

Follow the instructions.

Tips: Referencing electronic copies of papers

➤ Even if you find a journal on the web, you should reference it in your essay/ dissertation as if it were a hard copy of the article, giving the journal name, volume and page number, but not the web address where you found it.

➤ The one exception is for journals that are published only electronically (i.e. no hard copies are produced). There is a small but increasing number of these and they should be referenced in the same ways as websites (see Appendix 1).

3.4 Saving information effectively

Files and backing up

One of the important general skills you will learn at university is how to handle a mass of information and, most important, preserve it for future reference. Early on, you should have designed a provisional electronic filing system (see the section on filing in Chapter 2, pages 29–31). You also need to decide where you are going to keep it.

Tips: Backing up

➤ Never forget that laptops are not immortal: they crash, and get dropped and stolen. The chances are that, however shiny and new it is now, one of these things will happen to your laptop before you graduate. And it always happens at a crucial time, such as the night you finish an important piece of work that is due to be handed in the next day. You need a reliable and secure system for backing up. Set it up now.

➤ When you are working on a large piece of work over days or weeks, such as a final-year project or dissertation, avoid having too many copies of it floating around in different places. It is easy to get confused about which is the most recent version. It is best just to have one working file and one back-up file, onto which you put the contents of the working file every time you finish working on it. (This is of course especially important if you are collaborating on writing something, as we know from bitter experience.)

Ideally, you would store everything on your university server (see page 67) which will be backed up every night at no expense to you. If you mainly use university computers that is no problem; if you mainly use your own home computer, this is more difficult, but there will usually be a file transfer system for moving things between the university server and your home computer (see page 79).

A student's advice

☑ I was given an expensive new laptop to take to university and, despite leaving it lying around several times and even once having it in my digs when they were broken into, I still have it in my third year. I simply bought some indelible pens, scrawled my name and email address on the lid in large letters and covered every available surface with bad drawings (I can't draw anything else). It looked horrible, but it was never stolen.

Reference management software (aka bibliographic software)

There are now a number of sophisticated software packages that are specifically designed to store and handle collections of references to books and journal articles. The most commonly used and available are EndNote, Reference Manager and ProCite. They all now belong to the same company, the Thomson Corporation, which also runs Web of Knowledge (see page 73) and the signs are that it is now concentrating on developing EndNote rather than the other two. Another well-developed commercial package is RefWorks. These packages are now widely used by staff and postgraduates in universities, with EndNote probably being the most popular. They are expensive to buy but your university may have them site licensed for use free on university machines, and there is a national university discount scheme for buying them to use on your own computer. There are also several free or cheap packages available to download from the web, but these will not do everything that the commercial packages will do.

Good reference management software will do the following things.

• Create a personal database for your references together with abstracts, notes and keywords for searching.

- As well as typing references in, allow you to download them from databases, like Web of Knowledge and PsycINFO, with a couple of mouse clicks.
- Cite-while-you-write: the software can be linked to Word, or other word-processing software, so that references can be called up as you write, inserted in the text and built up into a full reference list at the end – all in the format (e.g. APA) of your choice.

This is amazingly valuable if you do not like proof-reading reference lists, but the software is probably only worth buying and setting up if you will be writing lots of essays and dissertations.

3.5 Plagiarism detection software

Screening coursework for plagiarism and collusion

The problem of people incorporating chunks of text from other sources, or even plagiarizing whole assignments and giving them in as their own work, has become ever more serious as the range of material on the web has increased and copying techniques have became very simple. (One year when marking assignments for one of our courses, we felt it would be more appropriate to price them rather than mark them.) However, the advent of plagiarism-detection software, such as **Turnitin**, now provides a very powerful tool for combating this form of cheating. We cannot emphasize enough that you must read things and put them into your own words, otherwise this will be picked up and you will be punished quite severely. It makes sense that people should be awarded a degree in recognition of the learning they have achieved and demonstrated in assessments, not because they stole them or bought them.

Tip: The real reason why you should not plagiarize

➢   Coursework is there to help you understand and remember material for future use. Plagiarized work achieves neither.

In order to use plagiarism-detection software, work has to be submitted electronically, usually through the VLE. The software then compares what you have written, both against material on the web and also work submitted electronically by other students in your own and other institutions. It then produces an estimate of the percentage of the submitted work that has been plagiarized and an annotated version of the work with links to the original sources. Turnitin has filters that can exclude genuine quotations and references in this comparison, so it will identify anything more than a short phrase that has been cut and pasted from elsewhere without identifying its source.

An example of an essay screened electronically for plagiarism and collusion

Figure 3.1 shows part of a student essay (also shown in Figure 4.1 with tutor's comments), which we submitted for electronic screening for plagiarism and collusion through Turnitin to give you an idea of how it works. It has been compared against other essays submitted to this software from universities across the UK, including the home university of the student, and with material on the web. Matches with essays from the home university if submitted at the same time would indicate collusion. Any other matches would indicate plagiarism.

The report is in two parts. First, there is an overall similarity rating (5% in this case) and a list of sources with which the software has identified matches. Then the essay is reproduced with the phrases that match highlighted with numbers beside them to indicate the source of the match. (The software has been instructed to ignore references and quotations, though see below.)

The lecturer or tutor will look at the overall estimate of similarity and then, if this is high enough to raise concerns, at the details in the essay. In the essay reproduced here, although there is an overall similarity rating of 5%, this comes almost entirely from quotations. Most of the matches are with essays from other universities that have included the same quotes. Because these have been put in single rather than double quotation marks, the software has been unable to identify them as quotations. However, they have all been attributed and so do not count as plagiarism. The two other matches, 5 and 6, are such short phrases that the similarity is just coincidental.

So this essay gets a clean bill of health for plagiarism and collusion.

Originality Report

Why do People Stereotype? by XXX XXX

From "PSYC120 Essay

Processed on 28-10-07 1:51 PM GMT   ID: XXXXXX   Word Count: 2309

Overall Similarity Index: 5%

Sources:

1   2% match (student papers from 15/03/06)

> Submitted to University of Aberdeen on 2006-03-15

2   1% match (internet)

> http://www.ideagrove.com

3   1% match (student papers from 06/12/06)

> Submitted to University of Derby on 2006-12-06

4   1% match (student papers from 08/11/05)

> Submitted to University of Wales, Bangor on 2005-11-08

5   < 1% match (internet)

> http://socrates.barry.edu/ssw-bbryson/SW646hiv/gay_stepfamilies.htm

6   < 1% match (student papers from 16/03/07)

> Submitted to University of Aberdeen on 2007-03-16

Text:

Why do People Stereotype?

The reasons for stereotypes and stereotyping have long been debated within Psychology,

especially within the field of social perception. Walter Lippman (1922) (cited in Cardwell, Clark

& Meldrum, 2000) was one of the first to tackle cultural and social stereotyping. Lippman felt

that stereotypes were; 'Pictures in our heads' that symbolised **2**   an '...ordered, more or less consistent picture of the world, to which our habits, our tastes, our

capacities, our comforts, and our hopes have adjusted themselves'.   He also felt

stereotypes had a fundamental role in cognitive and perceptual processes.

Social Psychologists Kratz and Braly (1933) (cited in Cardwell, Clark & Meldrum, 2000) built

on Lippman's theories and carried out studies to determine whether traditional 'social

stereotypes' as portrayed in the media were upheld and believed. They used one hundred

students from Princeton University. The participants were shown a list of ten ethnic groups

and asked to choose from another list of eighty-four words describing personality five words

for each group, which they felt were 'typical' traits of the group. Their results showed there to

be high levels of agreement between the participants, particularly concerning 'negative' traits,

even though the vast majority of students had never had interaction with many of the ethnic

groups in the list. This in turn suggests a strong indication stereotypes are reinforced by

media portrayal.

This early research links strongly to the field of Schema Theory, which has long been

considered and researched when investigating why people stereotype. A schema is our pre-

conceived ideas about the world; Fisk and Taylor (1992) (cited in Gross, 2002) believe a

schema to be 4   a 'cognitive structure that represents a person's general

knowledge about a given concept or stimulus domain'.   Schemas are thought by

many to be an important factor in stereotyping as they conserve cognitive energy, as they are

'automatic' thoughts which cause no effort to be exerted. We apply these cognitive 'blueprints' to a range of situations. This theory is supported by Augoustinos and Walker (1995). Also studies such as the one carried out by Buckhout (1974) highlight how our underlying beliefs or schemas can alter our memory of events as our expectations may override or have an influence on recall.

Another widely held belief, which links in with the reliance on schema, is that stereotypes are a consequence of cognitive short-cuts. Psychologists feel our attention is directed by stereotypes to help us manage in dealing with the huge amount of complex information we constantly receive from our social environment. Researchers believe there to be two kinds of short- cuts; Heuristics and Categorization. Heuristics are defined by Stratton and Hayes (1993) (cited in Gross, 2002) as 3 'Problem solving strategies which involve taking

the most probable or likely option... [Heuristics] provide a way of reducing a

complex task to a manageable set of tasks'. This explains how we apply cognitive

processes to organise tasks, to save time and effort. Heuristics can be split into two categories; availability, that is using information that is easily accessible from **long-term memory** (LTM), and representative-ness; which involves estimating the probability of something when it is weighed up against pre-conceived ideas about a group. Categorization is the processing and storing of information through division of new information into significant units for later reference. In other words people do not regard stimuli as if it is unique but rather process them through categorizing.

The Findings of a study carried out by Taylor et al. (1978) (cited in Gross, 2002) in which participants were asked to identify which member of a mixed group made a particular comment lends support to the theory that category stereotypes influence our recall rather than the individual. As the tendency was for participants to recall the category; i.e. black person, or women, as opposed to which individual made the comment. This shows that participants attributed comments to particular group members depending on their own expectations, rather than what was actually said.

The consequences of stereotyping are seen by many to be negative. Moghaddam (1998) highlighting this, with the view that stereotypes are '...generally inaccurate and systematically **biased**'. It is true to say stereotypes can fuel prejudices and lead to discrimination. For example studies by Duncan (1976) (cited in Taylor, 1999) in which participants were shown two men having a discussion that became heated, with one man shoving the other. The participants largely regarded the black man's behaviour to be more violent. This is especially true in the condition were the black man shoved the white man. Appear to strongly support this point of view. The study by Suedfeld et al. (2002) into the use of stereotypes during world war two surely provides some of the most disturbing and strong evidence for the negative effects of stereotypes. With peoples survival during the Holocaust coming down to whether they 'looked Jewish or not'. Other factors such as the Howard and Rothbart (1980) theory of negative memory bias and selective remembering, that is to say recall of facts critical to the minority group and the recall of facts that support our stereotypes, also fuel this argument.

5 **However it is important to note this view is not shared by all.** Allport (1954) (cited

in Gross, 2002) argued that stereotypes do actually contain a 'kernel of truth'. Similarly Asch (1952) believed that stereotyping was simply people's way of 'representing social reality'. Some Psychologists voice the opinion that many stereotypes can in fact be positive. Tajfel (1969) in particular went against the general (American) consensus and argued stereotypes are 'normal cognitive processes' Brislin (1993) (cited in Gross, 2002) supports this view

saying; 1 **'Stereotypes should not be viewed as a sign of abnormality. Rather, they** reflect people's need to organise, remember, and retrieve information that might

be useful to them as they attempt to achieve their goals and to meet life's

demands...'   For these theorists, stereotyping is not necessarily negative, but a means

by which the individual makes sense of their social environment.

Figure 3.1. Part of the essay shown in Figure 4.1, screened electronically for plagiarism and collusion.

4

Achieving good outputs

The formal, assessed work on your university course will take many shapes. It will be both written – in the form of essays, longer dissertations, practical and project report – and oral – in the form of presentations in seminars and other small groups. This chapter discusses each of these in turn, and considers ways of achieving the best possible results.

4.1 The purposes of assessment

Assessment of work of whatever kind that is submitted for marking or review will contribute in two different ways to your progress on the course. In the jargon, it can be treated as either summative or formative, or both.

Summative assessment

The marks from *summative* work will count towards your mark for the module and, if a module has more than one part, the marks will be weighted and added together to produce the final overall mark for that module. Supposing a module has a coursework essay weighted 30% and a final exam weighted 70%, then an essay mark of 75 and an exam mark of 65 will result in a final overall mark of 68%. Passing each component separately may be a requirement for passing the module but, in a practical module for example, good performance on one component may be allowed to compensate for poor performance on another. The final mark on a module will always be expressed as a percentage (see the box on page 17 for definitions of terms associated with a degree course). However, at some institutions the mark you get on your coursework will be on a simpler categorical scale. In the course of examining in various places we have seen 1–10, A–E and even the Greek letters α (alpha), β (beta) and γ (gamma) with, in the last two cases, lots of annotations with pluses and minuses. If your institution returns your work with marks on anything other than a percentage scale, find out how this is converted into percentages for producing the final module mark.

Marks for level 1 modules often do not count towards your final degree class. Marks in later years will start counting, and tend to be weighted more as you progress towards graduation. You will certainly have to pass those earlier in the course in order to progress into the following year, although you may be able to proceed to the next level while retaking a failed module from the previous year. There may also be a system for compensating one or two failures, particularly if they are near misses, to allow you to proceed. In some systems, particularly in Scotland, you may have to achieve a certain overall mark in order to get on to your chosen programme in later years.

Whatever course you are on, it is essential that you read your handbook carefully and make sure you have fully understood how the assessment scheme works. Assessment can be very mechanistic and it would be a pity to find yourself having to retake modules, or even a whole year, because you had not understood that progression was dependent on passing something. The rules are often very different from those you have been used to if you have been taking A-levels. Appealing against your mark is much more difficult, and retakes are normally limited to outright fails. You will not usually be able to retake an exam in order to improve on a weak pass, and when you retake a failed exam the mark may be capped at the minimum mark needed for passing.

Giving things in on time is also crucial. Marks will usually be deducted for late submission. It is no good expecting your tutor to get you out of a hole – they are bound by the system too. Enforcing coursework deadlines means that everyone has the same amount of time to complete the work, and ensures fairness. If you have an exceptional problem, follow the procedures in the course handbook for getting an extension.

Formative assessment

Formative work is done to help you improve your skills by giving you practice and feedback, but will not count towards the final mark. Most work is both formative and summative, but the emphasis varies. With formal exams the only specific feedback you will normally get will be the mark, but you may get some general advice on where all students went right and wrong. You can always try to get more by asking, but institutions vary on how much they are able to give. If you have 300 students taking an exam, it is difficult to give more than general feedback. With multiple-choice exams, you will usually only get the mark, and sometimes your answers and the correct answer sheet so at least you can see where you went wrong. Exams are therefore primarily summative, although if they do not count towards the final degree, as with first-year exams at some universities, they are also intended to be formative in the sense that they will give you feedback on how well you are doing, giving you a chance to focus on what you have learned so far and work on your technique before attempting the exams that really count.

On the other hand, with coursework like essays and practical reports, the formative element is as important as the summative. In the excitement of looking at the mark when your work is returned this is something that is often forgotten. The feedback is there to help you see how you can improve things next time (see the sections on feedback below, pages 102–111). If you do not get sufficient comments on your work for you to know why you were given the mark that you got, then try asking the lecturer for more. A common complaint in the National Student Satisfaction Survey is that feedback on coursework is often too skimpy or too late to be helpful. If you find this is the case, then ask your class representative to bring the issue up with the course team. Try not to be passive – give feedback on your feedback in order to 'complete the loop'.

Tip: Know the rules

➤ Check out the assessment regulations early on so that you know where to concentrate your effort.

4.2 Writing essays

Getting started

We have a motto in our household, borrowed from the American humorist James Thurber: "Don't get it right, get it written." If you are faced with an assessment task, it is all too easy to fiddle about and engage in various kinds of **displacement activity**, but the great thing is to make a start and then keep coming back to it. You will find that your brain has been quietly turning it over and, once you have got some idea of what is required, you may also pick up useful information while doing other things. This is why it pays to start writing more than 24 hours before the deadline. The glory of word processing is that an essay can remain fluid until you hand it in, so if you find new material you can always weave it in at the last moment, but always read the essay through afterwards to check for continuity. Picasso said, "Every morning I go into the studio and face a blank canvas", so you are not alone!

Here is a checklist of 'throat-clearing' things to go through when you are set an essay. At the least they will start you off on the right foot, and prevent you wasting time by running off in the wrong direction, or having to re-type your work before you give it in.

1 Look at the title carefully – what aspects are relevant? What is the verb that indicates the task set (e.g. 'assess', 'compare', 'discuss', 'evaluate', 'illustrate' all call for a different structure and approach).
2 If there are two parts to the question, be careful to answer both. It is quite common for a more evaluative question to be tucked in behind the initial one.
3 Check what word length is specified, if any.
4 Check if there are other formatting specifications – font size, margin width, line spacing, etc.
5 Check what system you should use for referencing (see Appendix 1). Even though there are accepted systems, institutions may vary in how they implement them.
6 Check the date and method of submission and how it relates to other deadlines. Lecturers are not always very good at liaising to spread the assessment deadlines, so you may well find that they are bunched, particularly at the end of semesters, which calls for careful forward planning.
7 Consider who will mark the essay and what their approach is likely to be.

If you cannot find the answer to any of these in course handbooks, handouts or on web pages, ask the person who set the assignment.

Helicopter view

One good way to start on the actual essay is by marshalling what resources you have already. Essay titles on a course rarely arise out of the blue. Try looking at your lecture notes and organize items around the essay title. The areas where you need to do more work on your own should start to become apparent. If you are not sure where to start, look at the recommended textbook or basic recommended reading to give you an overview, or look at an alternative textbook from the library to get a different approach to the topic.

Follow up any specific **references** from the lectures, from your tutor or from your textbook first. The point of being on a course is to have a guide to introduce the topic and point out for you the salient things to look for. If your lecturer provides you with clear, up-to-date references you will only need to search the literature independently when doing essays later on in your course, in order to put some original icing on the standard cake. Supplement these by checking anything basic you do not fully understand. You can do this on your own, by using an appropriate search engine, such as Wikipedia, or a dictionary of psychology (see Appendix 6).

Only then should you embark on a literature search of your own to fill in any gaps, find more information about very specific points or check for very recent developments (see also the section on 'References and finding your own sources', page 35).

To summarize:
1 lecture notes first
2 then course textbook
3 follow up references from lectures
4 check understanding
5 look up anything that is not clear in your mind
6 literature search to embellish a few specific points.

TOMtip

❖   Lecturers are human, too, with particular interests and views. Bear this in mind when writing an essay for them – not forgetting that they will also appreciate originality.

Collecting additional material

It is better not to embark on this until you have prepared the ground and know exactly what you are looking for. You can waste vast amounts of time and become completely overwhelmed with out-of-date, irrelevant material. The amount you have to do will depend on the nature of the topic, the coverage in your prescribed reading and the level at which you are working. A third-year essay or dissertation will require much more original material than your first essay in the first year. Annotate each item at the time so that when you come to write the essay you do not forget why it is significant.

There are many ways of finding additional material, and you will often come up with the same sources or different sources that cover the same ground, so you will have to be selective.

- *Advanced books:* there may be conference proceedings or monographs on your topic. Look in your library catalogue for something recent.
- **Journals:** the best way to look for journal articles is to use web-based databases (see pages 73–75). There are two kinds of articles you could look for.
  - *Review articles:* if you can find a recent review of your topic, this will save you a great deal of work.
  - *Research articles (reports of original studies):* these can usually be skim-read (see page 39) unless you are discussing the methodology used, but do not always accept the author's conclusions uncritically.
- *Web search engines (e.g. Google):* use as many carefully selected keywords as possible to focus your search, otherwise you will be overwhelmed! The 'Advanced Search' button on Google enables you to specify all the keywords in a specific order and stops it identifying things containing each word singly. Remember, there is no editorial control on the web and what you find may be brilliant or rubbish – it is up to you to decide (see the section on this in Chapter 3, pages 80–82).
- *Figures and pictures:* while you are reading, make a note of any figures, diagrams or pictures that you might want to use for your essay. A graph of results or a diagram of brain anatomy will often explain things more clearly than words. They also enable you to pack in more information without exceeding the word limit since they do not normally count against this. You can save figures from electronic articles to paste into your essay, and Google Images is a good source of additional visual material.
- *Personal websites:* an increasingly useful source of free up-to-date material is to visit the website of the psychologist whose research you are interested in. You will often find copies of many recent **papers**, and sometimes even teaching materials from their lecture courses.
- *References:* while reading, always make a careful note of the full reference so that you do not waste time having to go back to check it when you are compiling your reference section – inevitably at the last minute. (See Appendix 1 for more details on referencing, and page 83 for more on how to use referencing software.)

Tip: Illustrating your essay

➤ You are writing an essay on 'The role of the fusiform gyrus in face recognition'. Put 'fusiform gyrus' into Google Images and there is your Figure 1 (remembering, of course, to attribute the source).

Planning the essay

The plan, although essential, is not necessarily the order in which you should ultimately tackle the essay. It is sometimes helpful to write the introduction later on, so you do not become frozen waiting for the definitive summary to occur before writing the body of the essay. However, do write a plan first, and add short notes to remind you what goes where – but do not get bogged down in writing whole paragraphs at this stage.

Outline plan for an essay

Introduction
- Define the ground – what is the point of the question and why is it of interest?
- Are there competing theories that need to be assessed?
- Is there conflicting evidence?
- Are there recent developments?

Main section
- The content will largely dictate the structure, which is why it is efficient to do a plan first.
- Try to lay out an argument, rather than just give a description.
- If there are two viable sides to the topic, use 'On the one hand . . . but on the other . . .'.
- Another structure is to set out an explanation and then try to knock it down with questions.
- Include some original source material if you can.

Development and conclusion
- Where does this leave us?
- What is the answer to the question you are being asked?
- Are there problems with the methodology?
- What are the remaining questions?
- Can you suggest any ways forward?

References
- There are clear conventions about this which you should follow (see Appendix 1).

Tip: Using 'Find'

➤ When you are writing an essay, in order to keep the flow use '???' to mark things such as references, dates or further information that you need to check and come back to. Then use 'Find' in Word to go through afterwards taking them out and replacing them with the correct information.

Write in the right style

The convention in psychology is that essays are written in a formal style, so it is better to avoid using the first person (e.g. 'I think . . .') or apostrophes to abbreviate (e.g. 'didn't'). If you are not sure about the right tone, look at some examples from a psychology textbook or, better still, a research paper, but, above all, keep it simple and clear.

The BPS has a useful set of guidelines for using non-sexist and non-ethnically biased language (www.bps.org.uk).

You should also try to avoid vague or imprecise phrases such as 'Psychologists postulate that . . .'. This example can easily be sharpened up by adding 'such as x, y and z' after 'psychologists', or qualifying it with an adjective defining which theoretical persuasion of psychologists does this (e.g. 'behaviorists').

Tip: Avoid 'believes'

➤ In reporting evidence be careful about the verbs you use. Avoid saying someone 'believes that . . .', especially 'psychologists believe that . . .'. Unless that is what they have written, you can never know what somebody actually believes. Also it implies that it is an act of faith, not based on any evidence, so, unless that is what you do want to imply, avoid it. Instead say 'Freud (1906) argued that . . .', or, if it is a fact, 'Zajonc (1969) reported that . . .', or, if it is an incontrovertible fact, 'Hubel and Wiesel (1958) found/discovered that . . .'. Language is a subtle creature; use it carefully.

Never be tempted to make a scissors and paste patchwork of other people's writing. Always try to put material into your own words and never incorporate sections from elsewhere without attributing them. This practice can easily be detected by putting sections of text into Google, or using plagiarism-detection software like **Turnitin**, which will give the percentage of plagiarized material, the source and the actual phrases or sentences (see Figure 3.1 for an example), and you will be heavily penalized. Universities and colleges take a very strong line on plagiarism.

Use direct quotes only when:

* someone very important said something very significant
* the point is very surprising, and the exact wording is important
* the point is beautifully, succinctly or wittily expressed.

An example of the last would be these lines of Alexander Pope's:

> True wit is nature to advantage dressed,
> What oft was thought, but ne'er so well expressed.
>
> (Pope, 2004, l. 297–298)

Put quotes in double quotation marks or, for a longer quote (usually of about 40-plus words), in a separate indented paragraph, and always give the page number of the source as well as the reference. Full guidelines for referencing are given in Appendix 1.

Aim to vary the length of your sentences and avoid long, convoluted ones. Short sentences and paragraphs are a good way of providing emphasis. Use abbreviations, especially if you are writing to a tight time limit, but always spell them out, with the abbreviation in brackets afterwards – e.g. **intelligence quotient (IQ)** – the first time you introduce them. It shows you know what they mean as well as being stylistically correct. (See the section on 'Exam answers' below, pages 127–8, for more thoughts on writing clearly in exams.)

Good use of punctuation will also help to make your meaning clearer. If you are sceptical about this, consider the now famous example of the panda walking into a bar who, after asking for some food, 'eats, shoots and leaves' as opposed to 'eats shoots and leaves' (Truss, 2003). We quite often receive essays with virtually no punctuation, making them very difficult to follow. The pressure of university timetables may not always make this realistic, but checking your punctuation is very much easier if you come back to what you have written after a day or so.

TOMtip

❖ If you have time, put a printout of your work away for a day or two before reading it through again. This makes it easier to judge how it will appear to someone else reading it through for the first time. It can be surprising how a sentence that you thought was clear and elegant immediately after you wrote it, now looks opaque or clumsy.

Presentation

The usual expectation is that essays will be word-processed. Most institutions now have libraries or learning resource centres where personal computers and laptops are available (see Chapter 3 on IT). You will have to submit the work in either printed or electronic form, or both. Electronic submission is required if it is going to be automatically scanned for plagiarism.

Make full use of all the aids built in to word-processing software (e.g. Word), particularly 'spell check'. If your IT skills are not very advanced, see if you can find a course to help you at your learning resource centre or through the computer services department. You will find it is time well spent in the longer term. Assess what your essay will look like as a whole and try to make it user-friendly by dividing it into paragraphs, focused round different elements in the account.

Tip: Disability

➢ If you have a disability, it is often possible to get specialist advice or even a grant to help you buy appropriate learning tools and equipment. Visit your university's Student Advice Centre to investigate the possibilities, or refer to the website for Skill: the National Bureau for Students with Disabilities (www.skill.org.uk), and look for details of the specialist equipment allowance that may cover things you need to benefit fully from your programme of study, such as a computer, tape recorder or electronic Braille note taker, together with adaptive technology, training and cost of repairs. Aimhigher (www.aimhigher.ac.uk) will also help you with this.

Can you make your work look more attractive in overall outline? This might be achieved by adjusting the margins and length of the paragraphs, arranging the text so that tables or diagrams do not straddle two sheets, and avoiding odd lines of text at the top and bottom of pages.

TOMtip

❖ The assignment marking scheme may not have explicit marks for quality of presentation, but we are all biased in favour of something that looks attractive and well presented.

Tips: Improving your writing

➢ Turn the 'spell check' button permanently to 'on'.
➢ Make use of the editing function in Word.
➢ Print out a draft and read it through carefully – it is easier to spot minor errors on paper than on the screen.
➢ Read it through in different modes, first for meaning and style and then for **typos**. (These are different skills and it is almost impossible to attend to both at once, which is why publishers tend to employ editors to concentrate on meaning and style and proof-readers to correct technical points.)

If you want plenty of comments then print it out double-spaced and leave nice wide margins, even if your institution does not already insist on this. You will need more paper, but it will be well worth it.

TOMtips

❖ If you have just finished writing something, when you read it through top-down processes will often cause you to see what you thought you had written, rather than what you have actually written.
❖ If possible, get someone else not on the course to read it through for style and language errors.

Diagrams and figures are a succinct way of presenting detailed information, and very useful if you are writing within a strict word limit, but only include those that are of immediate relevance (see the section in Chapter 5 on presenting data effectively, pages 146–155).

Citing and referencing (or how to avoid plagiarism)

This is the boring but important bit.

- If you give a fact, always give the source if you possibly can.
- If you make an assertion or claim that is not your own, give the source.
- Distinguish between primary and secondary sources. A primary source is the place where an idea or result first appeared – usually a monograph or a journal article. A secondary source is one that re-describes that idea or result – for example, a textbook. If you have only read the secondary source, but want to refer to the primary source, this must be made clear in your referencing.
- See Appendix 1 for more detailed advice on formatting references.
- There is now excellent **bibliographic software** (see page 83) available for organizing references and creating reference lists as you write. Many institutions make this available on their **intranets** and may supply copies for you to put on your own PC at minimal cost. This is probably useful only if you are writing something very long like a PhD thesis or many articles on the same topic, as your lecturer probably does, but it might be worth considering. Take advice from your tutor.

Tips: Referencing

➢ Master the tedious detail about formatting references as early on in your course as possible, so that it becomes automatic as you write.

➢ Keep any advice you have been given on referencing in front of you when you write, rather than looking it up afterwards and finding you have to change everything.

➢ As well as using referencing guides like Appendix 1 and the *Publication Manual of the American Psychological Association* (2001), it is helpful to have a copy of an APA journal article beside you to act as a model. You can use this book too. We have tried to keep to APA rules – apart, of course, from the deliberate errors.

Making good use of feedback

The point of writing essays is to learn how to improve. The more feedback you can obtain, the better. Marks for essays early in the course do not usually count towards your degree class, but they are a very good way of checking you progress and developing your skills as a psychologist in using material and data.

Never just look at the mark, feedback is the best way of learning and improving your work. If your tutor offers written comments, go through them carefully, make sure you understand them and identify ways you should be doing things differently. Sometimes lecturers have developed sheets summarizing the most common mistakes that people tend to make, rather than writing individual feedback on essays. If this is the case, go through and decide which mistakes apply to you, or swap essays and do it with someone else.

Remember, though, that markers will vary in terms of the emphasis they place in their feedback – though hopefully not in the way they produce the final mark. Some may seem obsessed with your referencing, some with your grammar, some with the overall structure of your argument, and some with the information you have not included, despite the fact that you have already gone over your word limit. Evaluate all this thoroughly. It is there for your benefit and if you do not use it everyone's time has been wasted. You will find that, as in life, the amount and quality of the feedback you receive will vary. Notice who has done the marking and make a judgement about how seriously to take their feedback. If it is very thin, try going to the marker to ask for more. It may not be helpful, but it cannot do any harm.

Tips: Feedback

➢ When your coursework is returned to you and you have calmed down from the delight/distress of finding out what mark you have been given, sit down quietly and go through the feedback to see how you can do (even) better next time.

➢ Try swapping an old essay with someone else and marking each other's, giving comments, but do not do this until the essay has been marked and returned! Identifying how someone else could improve their work is one of the best ways of understanding how to make your own better. It will also help you to see if you really do understand the subject.

An example of a good first-year student essay with feedback comments

Figure 4.1 is an actual first-year essay, showing the comments from the lecturer when it was returned.

Why do People Stereotype?

The reasons for stereotypes and stereotyping have long been debated within Psychology, especially within the field of social perception. Walter Lippman (1922) (cited in Cardwell, Clark & Meldrum, 2000) was one of the first to tackle cultural and social stereotyping. Lippman felt that stereotypes were; 'Pictures in our heads' that symbolised an '…ordered, more or less consistent picture of the world, to which our habits, our tastes, our capacities, our comforts, and our hopes have adjusted themselves'. He also felt stereotypes had a fundamental role in cognitive and perceptual processes.

> **Comment [RML1]:** *Give page numbers of quotes if you can.*

Social Psychologists Kratz and Braly (1933) (Cited in Cardwell, Clark & Meldrum, 2000) built on Lippman's theories and carried out studies to determine whether traditional 'social stereotypes' as portrayed in the media were upheld and believed. They used one hundred students from Princeton University. The participants were shown a list of ten ethnic groups and asked to choose from another list of eighty-four words describing personality five words for each group, which they felt were 'typical' traits of the group. Their results showed there to be high levels of agreement between the participants, particularly concerning 'negative' traits, even though the vast majority of students had never had interaction with many of the ethnic groups in the list. This in turn suggests a strong indication *that* stereotypes are reinforced by media portrayal

> **Comment [RML2]:** *Not necessary unless it is unexpected, e.g. if they are physicists.*

> **Comment [RML3]:** *What about other indirect influences from family and friends?*

This early research links strongly to the field of Schema Theory, which has long been considered and researched when investigating why people stereotype. A schema is our pre-conceived ideas about the world; Fisk and Taylor (1992) (cited in Gross, 2002) believe a schema to be a 'cognitive structure that represents a person's

> **Comment [RML4]:** *Better to give an approximate date, or a reference to its first introduction.*

> **Comment [RML5]:** *You do not know what they believed, so say 'suggested', 'proposed' or 'argued that'*

general knowledge about a given concept or stimulus domain'. Schemas are thought

by many to be an important factor in stereotyping as they conserve cognitive

energy, as they are 'automatic' thoughts which cause no effort to be exerted. We

apply these cognitive 'blueprints' to a range of situations. This theory is supported by

Augoustinos and Walker (1995). Also studies such as the one carried out by

Buckhout (1974) highlight how our underlying beliefs or schemas can alter our

memory of events as our expectations may override or have an influence on recall.

Another widely held belief, which links in with the reliance on schema, is that

stereotypes are a consequence of cognitive short-cuts. Psychologists feel our

attention is directed by stereotypes to help us manage in dealing with the huge

amount of complex information we constantly receive from our social environment.

Researchers believe there to be two kinds of short-cuts; Heuristics and

Categorization. Heuristics are defined by Stratton and Hayes (1993) (cited in Gross,

2002) as 'Problem solving strategies which involve taking the most probable or likely

option... [Heuristics] provide a way of reducing a complex task to a manageable set

of tasks'. This explains how we apply cognitive processes to organise tasks, to save

time and effort. Heuristics can be split into two categories; availability, that is using

information that is easily accessible from long term memory (LTM), and

representative-ness; which involves estimating the probability of something when it is

weighed up against pre-conceived ideas about a group. Categorization is the

processing and storing of information through division of new information into

significant units for later reference. In other words people do not regard stimuli as if it

is *they are* unique but rather process them through categorizing.

The findings of a study carried out by Taylor et al. (1978) (cited in Gross, 2002) in

which participants were asked to identify which member of a mixed group made a

particular comment lends support to the theory that category stereotypes influence

---

Comment [RML6]: *Is this a quote from Fisk or Gross?*

Comment [RML7]: *too vague*

Comment [RML8]: *Say why, as you have with Buckhart, especially as this is apparently a primary reference (although I see it is not in the reference list!)*

Comment [RML9]: argument

Comment [RML10]: *The suggestion is that*

Comment [RML11]: *Yes, and true of the environment in general. Stereotyping is just another example of top-down processing influencing our perception of the world.*

Comment [RML12]: *Again true of perception in general. We see things faster if they fit easily into a category and we distort things so that they fit into pre-determined categories.*

our recall rather the individual. As the tendency was for participants to recall the

> Comment [RML13]: *Not clear.*

category; i.e. black person, or women, as opposed to which individual made the

comment. This shows that participants attributed comments to particular group

members depending on their own expectations, rather than what was actually said.

> Comment [RML14]: *I see what you mean, but this could have been expressed more clearly.*

The consequences of stereotyping are *usually* seen ~~by many~~ to be negative.

Moghaddam (1998) highlighting this, with the view that stereotypes are '…generally

inaccurate and systematically biased'. It is true to say stereotypes can fuel prejudices

> Comment [RML15]: *This is an interesting assertion. It suggests that we have evolved a cognitive process that is faulty. Given the nature of evolution, this cannot be right. The benefits must in some way outweigh the harm that the inaccuracy generates, otherwise it would not have been positively selected.*

and lead to discrimination. For example studies by Duncan (1976) (cited in Taylor,

1999) in which participants were shown two men having a discussion that became

heated, with one man shoving the other. The participants largely regarded the black

man's behaviour to be more violent. This is especially true in the condition were the

black man shoved the white man. Appear to strongly support this point of view. The

> Comment [RML16]: *This is not a sentence.*

study by Suedfeld et al. (2002) into the use of stereotypes during world war two

surely provides some of the most disturbing and strong evidence for the negative

effects of stereotypes. With peoples survival during the Holocaust coming down to

whether they 'looked Jewish or not'. Other factors such as the Howard and Rothbart

(1980) theory of negative memory bias and selective remembering, that is to say

recall of facts critical to the minority group and the recall of facts that support our

stereotypes, also ~~fuel~~ *strengthen* this argument.

However it is important to note this view is not shared by all. Allport (1954) (cited in

> Comment [RML17]: *Good.*

Gross, 2002) argued that stereotypes do actually contain a 'kernel of truth'. Similarly

Asch (1952) believed that stereotyping was simply people's way of 'representing

social reality'. Some Psychologists voice the opinion that many stereotypes can in

fact be positive. Tajfel (1969) in particular went against the general (American)

> Comment [RML18]: *But they may still be wrong and they may still be harmful, for example allowing people to be conned.*

consensus and argued stereotypes are 'normal cognitive processes'. Brislin (1993)

(cited in Gross, 2002) supports this view saying; 'Stereotypes should not be viewed as a sign of abnormality. Rather, they reflect people's need to organise, remember, and retrieve information that might be useful to them as they attempt to achieve their goals and to meet life's demands…' For these theorists, stereotyping is not necessarily negative, but a means by which the individual makes sense of their social environment.

A further explanation for stereotyping is thought to be illus~~iona~~ry correlations. Hamilton and Gifford (1976) suggest a correlation is perceived between two events when in fact there is no correlation, such as; petty crime and a travelling community, due to each event being unusual and therefore memorable. The two factors are then linked and classified as a stereotype for future reference. A person's mood should also be considered as a factor ~~to~~ *in* stereotyping, as research undertaken by Bodenhausen et al. (1994) makes a strong case for mood being linked to cognitive effort. They found participants in a 'good' mood less willing to make an effort to reduce stereotypes. This lacking motivation could be due to an unwillingness to jeopardise their feeling of being 'happy'.

> **Comment [RML19]:** *or there may be a correlation but no causal link, they just happen, by chance, to occur together.*

It is also believed a person's physical appearance is linked to why people stereotype and that psychological trait are attributed according to how they look. For example, people are quick to class overweight people as 'jolly' and people with red hair often get labelled as having 'fiery tempers'. Studies, such as those carried out by Dion et al. (1972) highlight the 'attractiveness stereotype'. When participants were shown photographs, physically attractive people were repeatedly attributed with attractive personal qualities. For example they were often labelled 'warm'. This theory could also be linked to the stereotypes held about age.

> **Comment [RML20]:** *And, interestingly, the more familiar we are with someone the more attractive they are rated. (The 'Mere Exposure' effect described by Zajonc.) This could be part of the mechanism for building 'in-group' stereotypes.*

Ageism holds some of the most prevalent stereotypes today, as it is inferred what a person is like by how old they are, and the general consensus is 'old' symbolises 'different'. This is highlighted by Bromley (1977) (cited in Gross, 2002) who suggests old people can be looked upon unfairly because they are seen as different to the 'norm'. As Jones (1993) (cited in Gross, 2002) comments; 'What other section of the population that spans more than 30 years in biological time is grouped together in such an illogical manner? .. .As a consequence, older people suffer a great deal … They are devalued in the community…' An effect of such stereotypes is negative repercussions, for example research by Levy suggests the elderly can internalise the views which in turn can cause problems to both mental and physical health.

> **Comment [RML21]:** *This is a western stereotype. In many other cultures age is associated with wisdom.*

Gender-stereotypes similarly can have a significant impact upon a person. For example a study by Huguet and Pascal (2007) highlights how gender-stereotypes influence academic performance. Their research provides evidence that girls under perform when led to believe tasks to be undertaken are simply measuring mathematical skills. Which links strongly to self-fulfilling prophecy, which is to say other people's image of us becomes our own.

> **Comment [RML22]:** *Good point.*

Having discussed many of the early theories and how they are interlinked, it is important to note more recent research in the field of stereotyping is of the vein that stereotypes do not just function as cognitive short-cuts but also assist major functions for society. Jost & Banaji (1994) (cited in Taylor, 1999) argue that there are at least

> **Comment [RML23]:** *Good*

three major functions to stereotypes; 'ego justification'; in which our own status is protected, 'group justification'; in which the status of our own group is protected, and 'system justification'; in which existing hierarchies status is upheld. Based largely on

> **Comment [RML24]:** *Good*

the work of Tajfel, the field of social identity theory takes the view that many social differences such as, age, ethnic origin, gender and status can all produce stereotypes. It is also believed people favour their own groups for a number of reasons, these include; beneficience and competence. Beneficience is the belief of

> **Comment [RML25]:** *beneficence*

our own group to be more kind and generous. Competence is the belief of our own group to be more successful and intelligent. In other words people stereotype as a

> **Comment [RML26]:** *Good point.*

way of increasing self-esteem. Individuals show positive discrimination in favour of their own 'in-group', which in turn reflects favourably on their being a member of that group.

As much research has shown, it should be acknowledged that stereotypes can greatly impact upon prejudices. However it is worth taking into consideration that statements such as 'They all look the same' do not necessarily stem from bigotry but rather due to a lack of interaction with a particular group. This links to the theory of out-group homogeneity effect (Quattrone, 1986, cited in Gross, 2002). Research has shown people see more differences in their own group; this could be due to spending more time with that group, as suggested by the in-group differentiation hypothesis (Linville, et al. 1989, cited in Gross, 2002). Also Ppsychologists such as Neuberg (1989) (cited in Taylor, 1999) suggest that stereotypes can be broken down as stereotypes are not the same thing as prejudices. They are inherently different in the fact that a prejudice is much more rigid, it has been shown prejudiced people do not acknowledge new information which conflicts with their beliefs, but rather label it as simply inaccurate or unusual. Whereas a person that believes a stereotype, can more easily change their attitude when presented with conflicting information. Neuberg (1989) believes cognitive interventions such as asking people to look beyond the stereotype and really focus on the individual is one way to weaken a stereotype. The results being more accurate information is acknowledged and attributed to others.

> **Comment [RML27]:** *And is probably in part a genuine perceptual effect.*

In conclusion, stereotypes are assumptions that are widely held about people due to their group membership and research has shown there are multiple reasons for stereotyping. Some of the main reasons people stereotype are due to; use of schemas, to save time and cognitive energy, and reliance on pre-conceived ideas and prejudices widely held within our own groups. Other related reasons include;

belief perseverance and expectations learned through our culture. The media also plays a large role in our perception of minority groups. Having discussed reasons for 'why' people stereotype, it is fundamental to note stereotypes are wide-ranging and varied and the emerging pattern is that it appears they are practically inevitable and largely context dependent. The implications of stereotypes are far reaching and play a significant role in areas such as education, where the self-fulfilling prophecy can have a profound effect on intellectual and social development. Students may be adversely affected due to both their own and their teacher's stereotypical views. This links to how we see ourselves and how we see others, which forms the individuals' social identity. Gender-stereotypes particularly related to education if adhered to can strengthen the divide between gender performances. Another important implication of stereotypes is they can be used to fuel prejudice, for example, racism, ageism, sex discrimination, and as history has shown lead to atrocities such acts as ethnic cleansing and mass genocide. In closing, it appears that stereotyping is a useful and necessary cognitive tool which allows individuals to more effectively make sense of their environment. In many instances, this has a positive effect, as it provides ready prepared structures which can be applied to various scenarios, saving time and effort. If relied on exclusively, stereotypes can lead to inaccurate perceptions and prejudice, but is vital in terms of encoding and organising the huge amount of social information we need to process.

> Comment [RML28]: *Awkward sentence*

References

Cardwell, M., Clark, L., Meldrum, C. (2000). Social Cognition. In M.Cardwell (Ed.), *Psychology for A Level (pp. 210-214)*. London: HarperCollins Publishers Limited.

Gross, R. (2002). *Psychology The Science of Mind and Behaviour Fourth Edition*. London: Hodder and Stoughton Educational.

Hilton, J.L., Von Hippel, W. (1996) *Stereotypes*. Retrieved October 23, 2007, from http://www.questia.com/googlescholar.qst?docId=5000321907

> Comment [RML29]: *A good set of references – see notes on minor points. The one mistake you have made in referencing is to use references in the text that are not picked up in the References section, presumably because they are secondary, but without saying where they are from.*

> Comment [RML30]: *If this is actually a journal article then give the full reference if you can.*

Huguet, P., Regner, I. (2007) Stereotype threat among school girls in quasi –

ordinary classroom circumstances. *Journal of Educational Psychology* 99 (3), 545-
560.

Madon, S. (1997) *What do people believe about gay males? A study of stereotype content and strength.* Retrieved October 23, 2007, from

http://www.questia.com/googlescholar.qst?docId=5001522815

RevisionNotes.co.uk. *Stereotypes and Stereotyping* n.d. Retrieved October 23, 2007,

from http://www.revision-notes.co.uk/revision/875.html.

Suedfeld, P., Paterson, H.,Soriano, E., Zuvik, S. (2002) Lethal Stereotypes: Hair

and Eye Color as Survival Characteristics During the Holocaust. *Journal of*

Applied Social Psychology 32 (11), 2368-2376.

Taylor, I. (1999). *Active Psychology.* Harlow: Pearson Education Limited.

> **Comment [RML31]:** *Put volume number in italics.*

> **Comment [RML32]:** *Use lower case in the title of journal articles.*

Overall comment:

A well-presented and argued account. You write well and are approaching the right

style for scientific writing.

Figure 4.1. The first essay submitted by a student in their first year of a psychology degree; the lecturer's comments are shown in side boxes; Corrections are highlighted and crossed through, with additions inserted in italics.

You will see that there are two main kinds of possible comment: those that are genuine criticisms (e.g. style, presentation, fact or argument) and those that are in a sense the beginning of a dialogue where the marker is giving their views in response to a point the student has made. The former will bear directly on the marking, the latter are formative. There will also be corrections to spelling, reference format, and so on. These will probably not be comprehensive, just indicative of the kinds of mistakes you are making. It does not mean that the errors that have not been corrected have not been noticed. All errors of this type will have some bearing on the final mark you get.

Writer's block

There is a well-worn path, followed by students everywhere, when you cannot quite bring yourself to engage with an assignment, and every time you feel you should be getting on with it, you allow yourself to drift off into some displacement activity. This is a classic avoidance technique and answering emails is one of the worst manifestations – there is a distinct benefit to working somewhere where you cannot do this. Sometimes it can be attributed simply to being overwhelmed by the amount of work outstanding, anxiety builds as time goes by and the situation develops into a crisis. You hope the resulting adrenaline will carry you over the threshold and galvanize you into action. Eventually you write the assessment overnight and give it in, knowing you could have done it so much better, or you miss the deadline, incurring penalties or even failing an element of the degree.

TOMtip

❖ Try using a 'power hour' in which the goal is not to finish the essay, but simply to work as hard as you can for one hour. Because it is manageable it can really get you going (and of course you might want to carry on).

Some simple strategies will help you to avoid writer's block. How do you think we managed to write this book?

Exercise 4.1 Avoiding writer's block

- Start by looking at the task for half an hour well before the admission date. Be very strict with yourself over this.
- Avoid any feeling that you should start at the beginning – it will probably be better to build it from the middle.
- Try applying some behaviorism: schedule some short periods of time at regular intervals, brainstorm and draw a mind map of everything you can think of that is relevant.
- Shape your behaviour by giving yourself small rewards along the way.
- Carry a notebook with you and jot down anything you come across that seems relevant. Can it be organized into coherent trains of thought?
- Now look up your notes and see if you can put some flesh on the bones.
- Try to get a rough draft down and then put it away and go and do something else like going for a walk or tidying up. You will find your brain goes on turning it over and, when you go back to it, your ideas will have matured.
- Another technique is to imagine you are explaining it to an intelligent person who is interested in hearing about the topic, and write as if you are explaining it to them.

Of course this is a recipe for curing genuine writer's block and assumes that you have actually done some relevant work!

4.3 Writing practical reports

These should be concise and formal in style, using plain language and short, clear sentences. Stephen Lea, at Exeter University, comments that:

> Students go through a phase of believing that this conventional structure of experimental papers is a wicked imposition by a crypto-fascist academic establishment irrationally wedded to a nineteenth-century scientistic concept of psychology, but in fact writers should be grateful for being given a clear and concrete task.
>
> (Lea, 1999, web page)

The traditional format for practical reports is as follows.

- *Title:* brief, elegant and informative.
- *Abstract:* always write this last so that it fits the report!
- *Introduction:* set out the general area, give a brief mention of previous research, explain what question you are trying to examine and how you propose to do it, outline the **hypothesis** to be tested, and end with your predictions.
- *Method:* this might include **participants** (it is no longer good form to use 'subjects'), apparatus, stimulus material, procedure, sampling and statistics, depending on the nature of the practical. Each of these sections should have a subheading.
- *Results:* you should report what you observed, depending on the nature of the practical – questionnaire, observation or quantitative measurement, for example – and present data diagrammatically whenever possible (see Chapter 5, pages 146–154). One important question is whether to report the descriptive statistics first and then, separately, report the statistical analysis (see Chapter 5, page 154).
- *Discussion:* this refers back to the introduction and considers how the results impinge on the questions raised. It should start with a brief summary of your results and end with your main conclusion(s). It may refer to new literature that helps to explain your results and offer some suggestions for future research.
- *References:* these should be in APA format (see Appendix 1) unless your department has a different requirement.

- *Appendices:* this is where you put material that is not essential for the main message, but may be useful for reference, like raw data or an **SPSS** printout. (If there is more than one appendix, then these should be numbered and listed on the first page of the appendices.)

Check whether all these sections are required. For early practicals you may be asked to include only some of them.

We have left the detailed discussion of reporting results to Chapter 5, on final-year projects, and you may want to refer to the section on 'Reporting and analysing your results' (pages 146–161) now, for examples of how to display your data effectively and some common errors in interpretation, particularly if you have been given an open-ended brief about what to do.

Tips: Practical reports

➢ Tackle practical reports as soon as possible, while the details are fresh in your mind.

➢ Make sure any tables or graphs have explanatory legends and axes are clearly labelled.

4.4 Giving presentations (or how to avoid death by PowerPoint)

Most courses now include presentations among the assessment methods. Everybody finds these a bit daunting, but thoughtful preparation and rehearsal in as realistic a situation as possible will stand you in good stead, and give you a very important skill that you will soon find yourself using when you graduate.

Planning

Think about the presentations you have been to and what made them easy to follow and enjoyable (or the reverse!).

The two major factors in success are quantity of material and time. Most people come unstuck because there is too much of the former and too little of the latter. A distinguished academic we know, renowned for the perfection of his lectures, had a 50-minute 'hourglass' made in order to practise them – but this is perhaps taking it a bit far!

Decide on:

- the most suitable visual aids
- how to make it interesting and relevant
- specified length when spoken.

TOMtips

❖   Think carefully about the level of knowledge of your audience and adjust your material accordingly. If it is too hard or too easy, you will rapidly lose their interest.

❖   Consider whether you find it interesting – if you don't, why should others?

Visual aids

There is an overwhelming tendency to use PowerPoint as the basis for presentations as this gives you an outline of prompts to follow, is very user-friendly and fun to construct, and gives very professional effects. Beware, however, of getting carried away; nothing is worse than a very busy presentation, with elaborate backgrounds and things flying in from all directions, which distracts from the content and limits your ability to speed up or slow down according to how you feel the audience is responding. To misquote Marshall McLuhan, 'It's the message, not the medium which counts.'

If you opt for a different method you will have the advantage of doing something novel! A friend went to give a paper at a conference, only to discover to her horror that the organizers had been sent the wrong PowerPoint slides by her office. She knew what she wanted to say so she carried on without them, but there was one diagram she was relying on to explain something, so she asked the audience to draw it for themselves on their programmes, following her instructions. Afterwards everyone told her how well they had followed her argument and how much they had enjoyed her session. The moral here is clear: active learning situations are preferable, so try to build in episodes of audience participation whenever you can, even if it is only 'think of an example of when x happened to you and share it with your neighbour'. Many PowerPoint presentations include too much on each slide – reading out what is on the slides does not make for a good presentation!

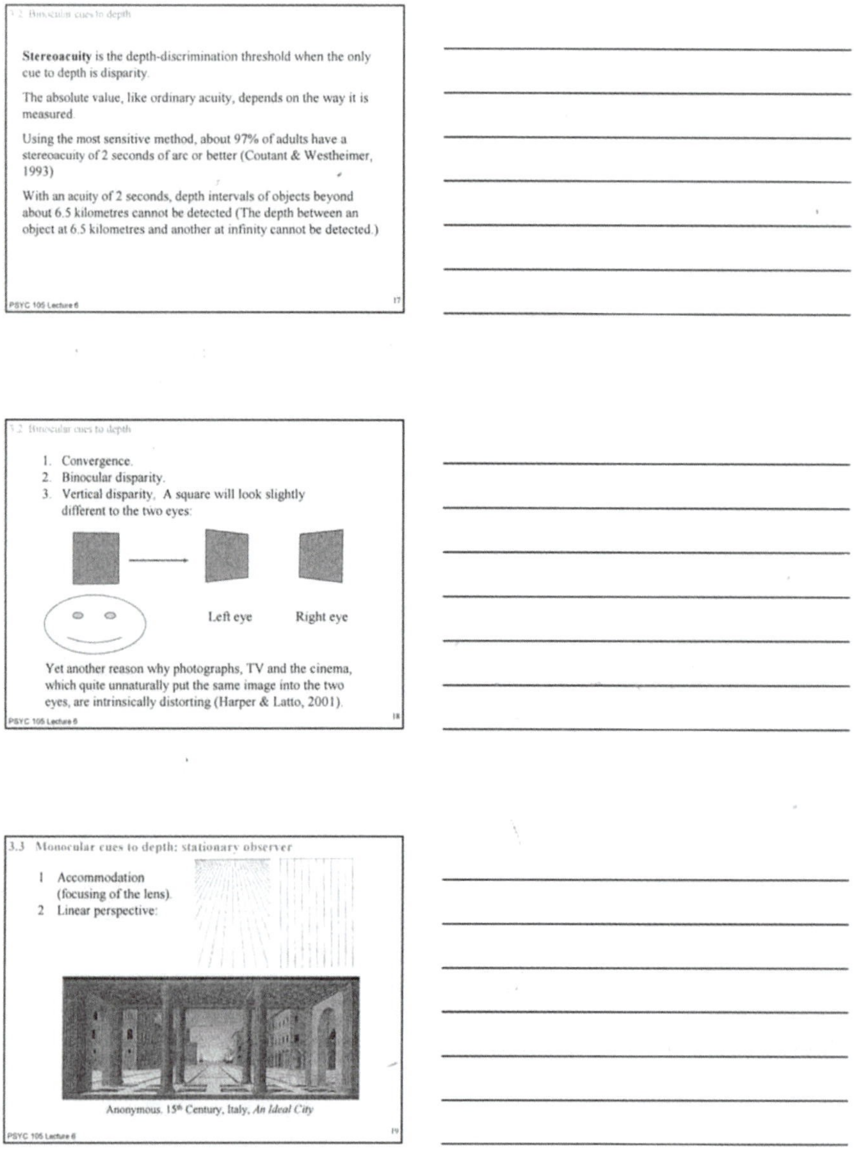

3.2 Binocular cues to depth

Stereoacuity is the depth-discrimination threshold when the only cue to depth is disparity.

The absolute value, like ordinary acuity, depends on the way it is measured.

Using the most sensitive method, about 97% of adults have a stereoacuity of 2 seconds of arc or better (Coutant & Westheimer, 1993)

With an acuity of 2 seconds, depth intervals of objects beyond about 6.5 kilometres cannot be detected (The depth between an object at 6.5 kilometres and another at infinity cannot be detected.)

PSYC 105 Lecture 6   17

3.2 Binocular cues to depth

1. Convergence.
2. Binocular disparity.
3. Vertical disparity. A square will look slightly different to the two eyes:

Left eye   Right eye

Yet another reason why photographs, TV and the cinema, which quite unnaturally put the same image into the two eyes, are intrinsically distorting (Harper & Latto, 2001).

PSYC 105 Lecture 6   18

3.3 Monocular cues to depth: stationary observer

1. Accommodation (focusing of the lens).
2. Linear perspective:

Anonymous. 15th Century, Italy, *An Ideal City*

PSYC 105 Lecture 6   19

Figure 4.2. An example of a PowerPoint handout with space for notes.

TOMtips

❖ Think of what happens in lectures – when you are reading lengthy material from a slide, are you giving full attention to what the lecturer is saying? Probably not.

❖ People have great difficulty in following two different messages in parallel. If you have a passage on a slide that you want the audience to read carefully, do not talk over it with different material. It is much better just to pause. This also helps emphasize the importance of the material.

Tips: Giving presentations

➢ Keep the number of slides down.

➢ Keep them simple – use diagrams, graphs, tables and bullet-point lists rather than text.

➢ Don't be tempted to reduce the letter size to fit in more.

➢ Leave slides up long enough for the audience to absorb them, and explain any particular points that may not be clear (e.g. what the axes of graphs are).

➢ Don't put important information at the bottom of the slide. Those at the back may not be able to see it.

➢ Build in some audience participation if you can.

➢ Don't be afraid to stop talking while the audience members read a quote or absorb a diagram.

➢ Practise with a watch – and an audience if possible.

On the day

Check out the room and the IT arrangements beforehand, especially if it is a room that is new to you, and try to have a dummy run with the equipment.

- Is your presentation compatible with the equipment?
- Can it be seen from everywhere?
- How do you change slides?
- Is there a remote control?
- Above all, interact with the audience.

Be clear at the start if you will take questions at the end or welcome interruptions, but do not allow the audience to take over – go back to your structure, saying 'I'm coming to that' if they anticipate you. You may also notice that experienced

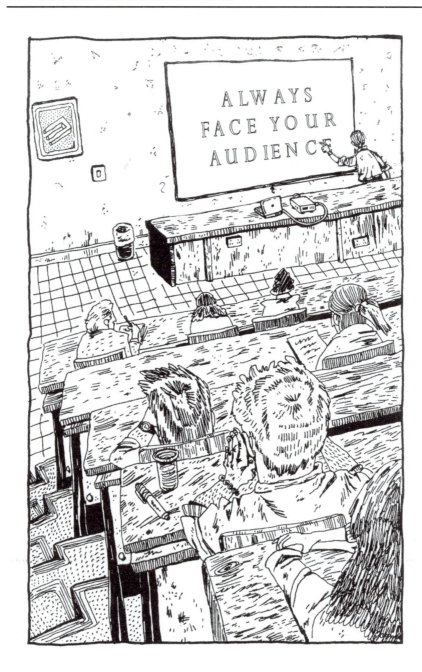

speakers have tricks for avoiding difficult questions – for example, 'That's a good question, can I come back to it at the end?' – hoping that by then the audience will have forgotten the question or that time will have run out. If you listen to politicians being interviewed you will recognize a few of these tricks, but you are not a politician and if you do not know the answer you can ask if anyone else in the room does and, if not, you can say that you will have to look it up. On the other hand, if you do know the answer, especially to a difficult question, it is impressive and worth allowing a short interruption, remembering how much time and material you still have left. Above all, never lose your cool with a questioner. Take printed copies of the slides with you (if the IT equipment breaks down this enables you to carry on) and use them out as handouts. The format shown in Figure 4.2, allowing for notes, is a particularly good one.

Students' advice on giving presentations

☑ Practise in front of an audience, however small.
☑ Keep the slides simple and avoid high-technology demonstrations unless you can check they work on the equipment you will be using.
☑ Relax, speak slowly and make eye contact with the audience.
☑ If you make a mistake, don't worry – the audience is on your side.
☑ Try to avoid just reading from a large page of notes or, even worse, from the slides.

4.5 Preparing and presenting posters

A good poster should be self-explanatory. Posters present an interesting exercise in synthesizing information and presenting it clearly, and make a good discipline for getting your thoughts in order. In a way, they would make good revision notes for exams. They are being used increasingly for presenting material at conferences or meetings, so doing one on your course will be useful preparation for later. Start early and give yourself plenty of time. You will probably change your ideas several times as you work it up and get a feel for the task. If you can look at any examples this is helpful. A web search will give examples of virtual posters. You can learn a great deal from looking around you at posters on the walls of your department and those in public places designed to give information, like museums and art galleries or even railway stations.

Tips: Poster presentations

➤ Check the required dimensions.
➤ Choose the software carefully (see page 72).
➤ Consider who the audience will be.
➤ Go for impact.
➤ Compile a list of headings.
➤ Think about visuals – photos, diagrams, tables.
➤ Design the overall structure to be clear and eye catching.
➤ Make the main heading large and clear so it can be picked out in a row of other posters.
➤ Use colour and typeface to distinguish headings and sections.
➤ Check the main text is readable from a distance.
➤ Try out a mock-up on a few people and ask them to assess it.
➤ Think about how you are going to transport it.
➤ Assess other people's posters.
➤ Use it to network.

If there is a poster session where you can stand by your poster, expand on the detail, answer questions and learn anything you can from people's responses, either about the subject or about your poster-production skills! A handout with further information and any references that you can offer to those expressing interest is a good idea.

4.6 Contributing to seminars

(See also the section on participating in seminars in Chapter 2, page 43).

The basic idea behind a seminar is to encourage you to participate and become an active learner, and you will be expected to attend. The format may vary – usually a student (or more usually several students) make(s) a presentation and others ask questions and comment, often turning it into a general discussion at the end. A seminar group will vary in size and is usually led by a tutor (although they may ask someone else to chair it). They will set out the ground rules, including specifying permitted visual aids and the time allowed for your input, and act as a timekeeper. However, the quality and value of a seminar depend largely on the students taking part. It is an opportunity to practise taking part in the kind of group discussion you will experience in many situations outside university. Make use of it – you will all benefit.

4.7 Taking examinations

If you do not like examinations (and that applies to most of us), it is better to tackle this issue right from the start. Do not put your head in the sand and hope they will go away: they will only loom larger as they draw nearer. A little forward planning will help you to feel more confident and do better. Find out from the student handbook (or web pages for the course) at what points in the course the examinations will be, which courses or modules they are associated with, and how the overall marks are distributed between different assessment tasks. A common pattern is for a module to have a mixture of assessment, perhaps an essay and an examination (see pages 91–93). An examination is the only method (apart from the very rare viva, mainly used at PhD level) for making sure that the work being assessed is all your own, so they tend to appear at important points in the course and feed significantly into your overall degree classification.

What is being tested?

When people think of exams, they tend to think of content rather than skills, but the content is only material for demonstrating the skills you have learnt, and it is these transferable, lifelong skills that will serve you well, long after you have forgotten all you have learnt. Of course, the catch is that you need to know the material in order to use it to demonstrate your skills.

Tips: Writing exams

➤ Exams are one of the few occasions left where you will have to write by hand without the benefit of spell check, so it is a good idea to practise.

➤ Some universities give you the opportunity to practise an unseen examination essay, perhaps in first-year tutorials. If they do, take advantage of it and take it seriously, especially if you are offered any feedback. It will pay off handsomely when it comes to the real thing.

Sadly it is often only after they have really sat down and mastered a topic for an exam that many students actually start to realize just how interesting it is!

You must be able to demonstrate a certain degree of knowledge in order to pass exams, but your ability to extract the important points and organize them to answer the question posed will be a key factor in the mark you receive. If the question begins with a word like 'evaluate', 'analyse' or 'criticize', you will be expected to do just that. This expectation will get stronger as you move through to the third year, so this is a skill worth practising from day one of your course. Psychology, perhaps more than most sciences, is based on foundations that are still developing and are therefore open to discussion and debate. By the end of your course, you will be expected to be able to take an intelligent part in that debate.

There are four distinct skills that tend to attract marks in examiners' marking schemes:

1 focusing your material in a way that shows you have understood the question
2 sticking to relevant facts, rather than regurgitating all you know on a topic; adding extra irrelevant facts will detract by making you seem vague rather than knowledgeable
3 reasoning, and organizing your material in a logical fashion
4 being clear and concise in your answer.

TOMtip

❖ Imagine you are your lecturer faced with marking 150 essay scripts, and think what will impress them.

Using past papers

Look at some copies of past papers to get a general feel for the format of questions. Lecturers are unlikely to set exam questions on topics not covered, at least to some extent, in lectures, so pay attention to coverage of topics in current lectures rather than historic exam papers. Looking back over the papers set on a course over a number of recent years will probably give you an indication of the topics that turn up regularly, but it is not a good idea to count on this. You should reckon to revise roughly twice the number of topics as there are questions on the paper. So, for a very common format of three questions in three hours, you should be armed with at least six well-mastered topics. Question spotting from past papers or comments the lecturer makes is sensible, but only up to a point: 'The question I expected didn't come up' will carry no weight with your examiners. Practise writing a plan and an introduction for all the past questions on the topic you are revising in, say, 20 minutes each.

Exam formats

Make sure you know well in advance, and certainly before you start revising, what format the exams will take. Common forms include:

- essay-type questions with no reference material
- set tasks or problems where a statistics book and a calculator are allowed
- multiple-choice questions
- open-book exams where the student may take in notes or other reference material
- 'seen' tasks where the student has prior warning of the nature of the task and can prepare for it.

Find out how many questions you will have to answer, and over what length of time. So many students now use word processors for all their written work that they are out of practice when it comes to writing fast (and legibly).

As always, if you really cannot find the answer to these questions, ask.

Revision timetable

It is a good anxiety-reducing tactic to draw up a revision timetable. Start early, calculate the time you have available and the number of papers you have to revise for, and divide your time up equally, unless you need to allocate more time to subjects you find more difficult. Avoid spending a disproportionate amount of time on a 'favourite' subject. Programme in breaks and rewards, and stick to them, making sure you get enough sleep (see page 124). An hour well organized and spent is worth more than two in an exhausted flap, and feeling in control of the situation will help you to stay calm. Exams seem to bring out extreme forms of gamesmanship, so take no notice of what other people say they are doing, or not doing, just concentrate on the tasks you have set yourself. Finding a quiet place to work in a non-psychology environment might be an advantage, unless you need specialist reference books.

Tackling revision

Tips: How to start planning your revision

➤ Look at how your material is organized and see if you can make it simpler and clearer.
➤ Fill in any gaps in your material or understanding.
➤ Identify things you don't understand, and ask.

> ➤ Have a look at the format and kinds of questions in past exam papers.
> ➤ Find out if there are any revision sessions offered by your tutor.
> ➤ See if you can identify a study group and revise together.

Revise by reading through your notes (see 'Notes on notes', pages 31–35) and jotting down the key facts on a topic. Some people find that using index cards helps at this point as they can be reshuffled in constructing answers to different questions. This is the moment to get help from your textbook or your tutor if you realize there is something you do not understand. If you are stuck, you could try   http://www.revision-notes.co.uk/University/Psychology/index.html,   but never forget that you will remember notes you have made yourself much more easily.

Trying to explain something to someone else is a very good test of whether you have really understood it, so revising in pairs or groups is a good strategy, but do not panic if they seem to know more: it might be an illusion. Practise answering questions under exam conditions, sticking strictly to the time limit. Like everything in life, performance improves with practice and exams draw on rather different skills than more leisurely essays. At most universities you will, for example, normally have to hand-write continuous prose without the help of any electronic editing facilities. The day when every student can have a computer in the examination hall will come, but not for a year or two yet.

Tips: How to revise

> ➤ Structure your revision, perhaps by practising:
>
>   ○ summarizing key facts and names on a topic
>   ○ listing the evidence for and against the theories and concepts you might be asked to evaluate
>   ○ producing skeleton outlines for different answers
>   ○ writing to time limits.
>
> ➤ Some general questions to ask yourself about the topic when revising:
>
>   ○ Outline and contrast two theories on . . .
>   ○ What is the significance of X's theory?
>   ○ Which psychologists would you mention in discussing . . .
>   ○ What methods could you use to study . . .
>   ○ What are the implications of . . .
>   ○ Evaluate Y's theory of . . .
>   ○ What is the evidence for . . .?

It is an awful truth that you cannot revise what you have not already learnt, so the more you have been an active learner, and the better your study skills and learning strategies have been during the course, the easier it will be to tackle your revision.

Learning has been one of the most studied topics in psychology and we have already mentioned some of the research on active learning and putting things in your own words – all highly relevant to university study – in Chapter 1. Another area relevant to student life is the importance of sleep. There is a large literature showing that sleep deprivation impairs both learning and recall (for example, Stickgold, James, & Hobson, 2000). More surprisingly, there is some evidence that a good night's sleep helps strengthen the memory for material learnt the day before – that is, performance is better in the morning than it was just before going to sleep (Born, Rasch, & Gais, 2006; Macquet et al., 2000). We can probably cope with short periods of sleep deprivation without too great a cognitive loss, but it is better not to build these into your planned timetable.

Having learnt everything effectively, you will of course have to recall it under exam conditions. Stress has a general effect on our ability to recall. However, the good news is that recall is, like many other skills, subject to one of the oldest and most robust laws in psychology, the **Yerkes–Dodson Law** (Yerkes & Dodson, 1908), which shows that, up to a point, stress actually improves recall, you just have to be sure that it does not increase too much (see Figure 2.3). Other, more specific, influences have also been discovered about the properties of the kind of **free recall** needed in exams. It is, rather worryingly, something that we are not always very good at – certainly not as good as we are with **recognition memory**. Importantly, a **state-dependent memory** phenomenon has been discovered. This suggests that matching the context of the original learning to the context of the recall improves the quality of the recall. This applies to both the emotional context – we remember things better if we are recalling them in the same emotional state as they were learnt (Ucros, 1989) – and to the physical environment. Godden and Baddely (1975), for example, tested the recall of two groups. One had done their learning on land, the other had done theirs 20 feet under water. They were then tested in a free recall situation in either the same or different environment. Recall was about 50% higher when the testing was in the same environment, so try to create a quiet revision environment that will match the examination hall situation, and practise writing exam answers in a similar environment. And it is probably advisable not to do your revision underwater.

Study groups

The stereotype of people revising for exams is of students alone, burning the midnight oil, but it does not have to be like that. Revising in a group of

friends can be very effective and will help you to concentrate on organizing and reorganizing material to answer different questions. Some lecturers may organize more formal revision sessions to do the same kind of thing. Take advantage of those as well.

During an exam

Look carefully at the exam clock in Figure 4.3 and memorize the stages you should go through at the beginning. Having a well-rehearsed ritual is a good way of avoiding panic as you turn the paper over.

How to avoid panic

- Start by reading the instructions. How many questions have to be answered? Is it a free choice from among those offered, or is there a compulsory question with a suggested time allocation? If so, you should always follow this, it will reflect the allocation of marks on the paper.
- Read the questions carefully. Avoid opting immediately for one because you recognize the content, without considering exactly what you are being asked.
- Ring the verbs (e.g. 'evaluate', 'contrast', etc.), and consider the material and structure required. If asked to compare, do not just give two descriptions, make sure you assess one against the other.
- Underline the terms that define the answer (e.g. 'according to Piaget', 'recent research').

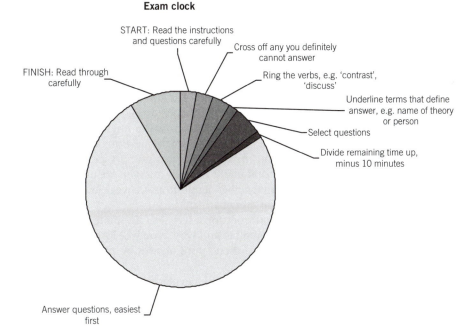

Figure 4.3. A suggested plan for allocating time during an essay-based exam.

- Cross off any questions you definitely cannot answer and then select from the remainder.
- Now check how much time is left and divide it equally into the number of questions, saving ten minutes for reading through at the end. Note the times at which you should move on to the next question.
- Do the easiest question first but stick to the time allocation, and do not be tempted to embroider.
- Read through your answers carefully in the last ten minutes to catch any silly mistakes.

Exam answers

The emphasis in an exam should be on demonstrating your command of the topic through your grasp of the details, and the force and cogency of your argument. While you might spend some time perfecting your style when writing an essay, here the issue is to cover the ground in a clear, simple style. Practising writing exam answers to time is an essential exercise, especially if you have composed all your essays on a keyboard. It makes the task more familiar and avoids panic.

Some students seem to find it difficult to grasp that there are marking schemes for each paper that allocate marks for each question. The idea is to assess the breadth as well as the quality of your learning. The first ten marks allocated for each question are the easiest ones to obtain, and the last ten marks the hardest. You will get zero for any questions you do not attempt. The obvious strategy therefore is to equalize your effort across the paper. Unless it explicitly says otherwise, marks are usually equally distributed across the questions. An exam paper requiring you to choose three from a number of questions to answer will give 33% of the marks to each. If you answer only two questions, perfect answers will still give you only 66% of the total marks possible and you are quite likely to fail. Make sure you attempt the right number of questions – a weak answer may be worth 20–30 marks more than no answer at all.

The same argument applies within questions. If it says 'Evaluate two theories of emotion, and say which is more credible and why', you will lose all the marks allocated to the last part if you forget to end your answer by picking the most credible and giving your reasons.

Try to avoid trite assertions without supporting evidence. The following are real examples from recent papers.

Example 1

'Visual processing is a complex process.' This does not mean much unless it can be followed with something to back it up; for example, 'over one-third of the cerebral cortex of humans is concerned primarily with processing visual information and another third has some role in this.'

Example 2

'Psychologists are very interested in the effects of social context on eating behaviour' is OK if you go on to say, 'in 2007 the Web of Science lists 230 articles on the topic'.

Example 3

'It has frequently been said that . . .' is OK only if it is followed by a few names of psychologists who said it.

Last resort in exams

If you have really failed to manage your time in an exam and it has almost run out on you, a last ditch strategy is just to write notes on the last question, in the hope of gaining a few marks – but avoid getting into this position if you possibly can.

The role of external examiners

It is a requirement that all university degree programmes in the United Kingdom have one or more external examiners. These will be respected, usually senior, academics from another psychology department. Their main function is to ensure that standards are roughly comparable across institutions. They see a sample of students' work and write a formal report on both this and on the fairness of the exam process as a whole. This goes (in principle at any rate) to the Vice-Chancellor of the university and is a very important part of the quality control system. Departments have to take what external examiners say very seriously, and so should you.

Some thoughts from recent external examiners

- Exams are an opportunity to tell your examiners what you know, and to demonstrate your ability to write clearly and develop an argument.
- Look at the question very carefully and spell the names of psychologists mentioned in the question correctly. In a recent exam, two out of eleven answers on the Stendhal syndrome spelt his name wrong all the way through. This rather detracts from the rest of the answer, however good!
- Spread what you know across the questions. I have just marked an exam paper where the candidates had to answer two questions on a third-year module on quite a narrow topic. The candidate put everything they knew into their first answer, getting a good first-class mark. The problem was that this left very little to put into the second answer, and much of this was irrelevant, so this got a poor third-class mark. Balancing the material better would have pushed the average up considerably as marks are allocated to specific questions and there is no compensation between different elements on an exam paper.
- Base your revision on the lectures and essential reading, but novel material or even a controversial argument will impress the examiner (and come as pleasant relief after reading 48 consecutive regurgitations of the lectures), so try to find some extra material on each topic you revise.

Multiple-choice questions

Many universities now use these as a method of assessment, particularly in the early stages of the course. They will often involve marking up a machine-readable sheet with your answers. Try to familiarize yourself with the particular procedure your institution uses, and always check carefully before you leave the examination room that you have completed everything.

Multiple-choice exams provide general feedback on how much you have learnt and understood, both to you and to your lecturer. There are very clear strategies that pay off here.

- Go right through the paper first of all and answer all the questions where you are confident about the answer. There is usually adequate time allowed, but this ensures that you get a shot at all the questions most likely to be correct first.
- Go back and make informed guesses where you are less certain of the answer. First, eliminate any choices you know to be wrong and then choose between the remainder.
- Lastly, if you are completely stuck, just guess. If there are no penalties for wrong answers, simply by responding where there is a choice of four, you have a 25% chance of getting a mark. Even if there *are* penalties for wrong answers, sometimes called negative marking, it usually pays off to have a guess. If there are four alternatives and you are pretty sure one is wrong then you have a one in three chance of getting it right by guessing.

Of course these last two strategies will not help you in terms of feedback about what you know, but they will help get you the best marks.

Orals and vivas

In these days of large intakes to psychology courses you are unlikely to encounter these, and certainly not until the third year, or even at the end of your course or PhD. In any case most psychologists would argue that they are not a fair way of assessing ability. They have sometimes been used in the past to confirm a degree class if someone has done very well and the department is considering whether to give them a first-class degree, or if their results sit on the borderline between two degree classes, or if there are special circumstances. They are typically run by the external examiner for the course who comes from a different university and whom you probably have not seen before. They are not about trying to trip candidates up. The questions are likely to be fairly open-ended rather than simple checking of facts, and the same rules apply as for answering exam questions: candidates should try to present a clear, rational argument and use any facts that come to mind. The examiner might follow up something written on an exam paper or essay to try to judge the candidate's clarity and depth of knowledge on a subject. Nowadays you are most likely to experience a viva when you come to do a research master's or a PhD where the viva is based around the candidate's dissertation, and it forms a central and valid part of the examination process.

Note that these are not to be confused with interviews that may follow suspicion of plagiarism, faking of data or other forms of cheating. In these the candidate will be pushed very hard on their sources and their evident knowledge of the topic (see also the section on plagiarism, pages 84–90).

Afterwards

When you come out of the exam and try to judge how well you have done, remember that everyone else has had the same tricky paper, has had to answer the same questions under the same stressful conditions, and that is what you should compare your performance against – not how well you would have done given the infinitely more relaxed circumstances in which coursework essays are written, with time, notes and creature comforts.

Re-sits

If you do drop a stitch in the knitting, it is usually possible to re-sit the failed element at a specified point in the course, but you may have to re-sit all the assessment tasks associated with that module. In the worst case you might have to take a year out and elect to re-take assessments, either with attendance or without, providing of course that you have demonstrated elsewhere that you have the ability and motivation to succeed eventually. You should discuss this very carefully with your tutor.

4.8 Overall thoughts on assessment

Assessment is key to a degree course, whether in psychology or some other subject. In formative mode (see the section on formative work, page 93), it pushes students to engage actively with the subject material and digest it, so they can use it and apply it to different tasks and situations. Assessment provides feedback both to students themselves and to their lecturers on how they are getting on, and highlights those areas that have been poorly understood.

In summative mode, it enables the university to make an assessment of how well a student has done, in as fair a manner as possible and over a range of different tasks. Examinations will always be with us as, with the possible exception of vivas, they are the best way yet discovered to ensure that the person receiving the mark is the person who has done the work.

The most common reason for students getting into difficulties (apart from simply not doing any work) is a failure to comply with the course assessment requirements – the main point of which is to make assessment fair and even-handed – so do make sure that you have understood what you have to do and by when. Assessment regulations make poor bedside reading, but you ignore them at your peril.

There is continuing discussion in academic circles about moving to a grade point average system as in the United States, where the assessment comes, like the course, in bite-sized chunks. This has not yet gained the ascendancy in the UK, where the view that assignments attached to each module should be balanced by periodic exams still prevails.

One thing is clear, regardless of how clever you may be, good organization, forward planning and an active learning stance throughout the course will stand you in good stead.

5

Research projects and dissertations

If you are taking a degree programme accredited by the British Psychological Society (BPS) you will undertake a research project or research dissertation in your final year. This is your opportunity to demonstrate your ability to work independently in an efficient and effective way. It will contribute a significant percentage of marks towards your final degree class, and requires careful planning and execution. It may also be important in deciding what to do next and could play a part in getting a place on a postgraduate course in psychology. This chapter will help you make a success of it.

5.1 Planning your timetable

Time is likely to be one of the biggest issues you encounter with your project, and particularly so if it involves collecting data in an environment outside the department that is not geared to your needs. Many potentially good projects do not get marks as high as they might because the student has not spent enough time on the final stages required for bring the report up to the standard of presentation required – usually that for a **journal** article. Swimming galas, nativity plays, inspectors' visits, illness and staff holidays always appear when most inconvenient, and as a visitor in another working environment all you can do is smile and lump it. There may also be bits of bureaucracy at the university end, such as getting the necessary clearance and **ethical approval**, which can hold things up considerably (see the section entitled 'Before you start', page 135, for further details of these).

A helpful exercise is to look at the timetable given in the course outline, focus on the handing-in date, and work backwards, remembering that there will be many other pressures on your time at this stage of the course. There will probably be specific course deadlines set for stages in setting up the project, starting before your final year, and the timetable of formal milestones might look something like this:

Planning	1 introductory lecture and discussion
	2 project application form, leading to the allocation of a supervisor
	3 agreeing a research question
	4 project synopsis
	5 final project outline (protocol) for obtaining ethical approval
Data collection	6 progress report form
Writing up	7 seminar presentation (this may be part of the formal assessment and contribute marks to the overall assessment)
	8 submission of drafts to your supervisor
	9 submission of the final report

Each course will have its own way of managing this and you should check very carefully what the precise requirements and dates are for your course – we are only trying to give you a general indication of how it works. These milestones are not just set to make sure you are getting on with the job. Comments from your supervisor or during a seminar discussion can play a very useful formative role in developing the project before you commit yourself by collecting the data or thinking about the analysis. If these stages are not set formally by your department, then include them in your own personal schedule. In our experience, a small pilot to test out your plan for data collection, whether it is laboratory or field based, while there is still the opportunity to modify things is well worth it. So build in some time for this too.

It should be immediately obvious that anything you can get on with in the way of a literature review, or even data collection, during the summer vacation before your final year will pay huge dividends.

Let us consider the process in more detail.

5.2 Choosing a topic

Tips: Some questions you could use in helping you to identify a project

➢ Is there a lecture course you have particularly enjoyed?
➢ Was there anything arising from a placement that offers an opportunity for further study on a realistic scale?
➢ Is there a lecturer in the department whose work particularly interests you?
➢ Is there some issue from outside the course that would benefit from the application of a psychological research technique?

Before you start

At some point during your penultimate year you will begin the process of being allocated to a supervisor for your final-year research project. It is worth engaging with this process promptly. The detailed rules will vary from institution to institution, but the end of the process will be the identification of the person you will be working with as your supervisor in the final year. Different supervisors and, particularly, the areas they work in, will be more or less popular. Departments have to spread the teaching load across all staff, so if you opt for a popular area you may well not be successful in getting your first choice of supervisor. If this happens, treat it as a challenge. Find out as much as you can about the allocated supervisor from the web or elsewhere, and be open in your discussion with them about what you are going to do. The success or otherwise of the relationship with them will be an important factor in the overall delivery of your project. Like all relationships, there is a responsibility on both sides to work at it. We have plenty to say about managing this relationship in later sections.

The pattern of student projects varies enormously both between and within institutions. You may find yourself working largely independently on a research area of your own devising. You may be given a promising but un-thought-out idea by your supervisor to try to develop into something workable as a longer-term research topic. You may be working in a group of one or two other students on a carefully planned programme of research mapped out for you by your supervisor. You may seem to be working as your supervisor's research assistant running a pre-planned study that is part of their research programme, and that, if it works well, may be published as part of that programme. Academic staff often take advantage of student projects as pilots for testing out ideas and methodologies.

Each of these different kinds of project has its advantages and disadvantages. On the one hand, something of your own devising may seem more fun, but it is also higher risk: your supervisor may not be able to give you well-informed advice, an unforeseen problem in collecting the data may arise, you may end up with un-interpretable results, or you may find halfway through that someone else has already done your study. On the other hand, doing something largely pre-planned by your supervisor is safer in that you will be doing something that is likely to produce useful results and that requires a different, though very valuable, set of skills. You will be working closely with your supervisor on a shared project, so you will be operating more on the level of colleagues than supervisor and student. A group project involves yet another different set of skills.

Anything involving patients or children will add an additional layer of time-absorbing bureaucracy in arranging things like Criminal Records Bureau (CRB) registration (see page 168) or NHS ethical approval (see page 144) or Statements of Collaboration for joint projects. Using student participants may seem less exciting, but is much more straightforward, especially if your institution has some kind of credit-gaining Experiment Participation Schemes for first-year students (see page 57), and will ensure that you obtain reasonable numbers of participants.

The important thing to remember is that it is possible to succeed, or fail, on any kind of project. You will just need to adjust your planning and execution to match the demands of the particular project to which you are committed.

Being realistic

After you have been allocated a supervisor, the next stage is to agree with them what you will be working on and to begin the process of narrowing down the question you will be addressing (your research **hypothesis**) to something that is both realistic and practicable. One of the most common errors we see year after year in final-year projects (and equally with PhD research) is being unrealistic about the potential scope of project that you can manage. It is no use having a fascinating and important question if there is no way in which you can generate the information needed to answer it within the resources available. If you are planning to do experimental work or elaborate fieldwork you should also consider the potential timetable very carefully – life has a way of thwarting project ambitions, so making sensible judgements about what is realistic is a significant part of demonstrating the ability to work independently and effectively. This is one of the important areas where you should seek the advice of your supervisor and respect their judgement. They will have valuable experience of research in general, and student projects in particular.

Unless you are offered a pre-planned study by your supervisor, this initial stage of agreeing a research question will be an iterative one. You will decide on a general area, find some relevant **references**, perhaps suggested by your supervisor, and read them through looking for specific questions that you can work on. It is also worth finding out if there are copies of projects in the same area that you could look at, especially ones given high marks. (The supervisor may have some, or they may be kept in the library or in a department archive.) You will then go back with these ideas to your supervisor, who will comment on them, perhaps sending you back to fine-tune them or do some more reading. This process may go through several repetitions until you are both agreed on the question you will be attempting to answer.

Some advice from students on choosing projects

☑ If you are particularly keen on a particular topic or area, find out what the rules are for allocating topics early, but don't be afraid to ignore them and talk to staff and organizers. It never does any harm to look keen.

☑ If you don't get the project you wanted, don't worry. I wanted to do something in social psychology, but was landed with a lab experiment on language perception. Although I still don't find the topic gripping, I did find the whole business of organizing and running an experiment interesting and, by working hard, I still got a first.

☑ After I had been allocated a supervisor and we had talked about some possible areas, I looked at some previous year's projects in similar areas, which gave me some ideas about what was possible.

5.3 Making the most of your supervisor

The relationship with your project supervisor is one of the two key relationships you will have with members of academic staff during your degree. Arguably your supervisor is as important as your tutor, especially if you are planning to make your career in a field of psychology related to the project.

TOMtip

❖   Ask yourself what attributes you would like to find in someone you were supervising, and try to steer a middle path between going off on your own and failing to consult until you are really in difficulties, and knocking on their door every morning.

It is in your own interest to meet the formal deadlines at the different stages (see the first section of this chapter, on 'Planning your timetable'), and 'manage up' by formulating your requests for help very succinctly and clearly so that you cover the relevant ground at each meeting with your supervisor (better still if you can email this in advance, so they have a chance to check things out before you meet). Academics tend to have much else on their minds and helping them to help you will be much appreciated

---

Student advice

☑ It is a good idea to take a note of any questions you want to ask with you to a meeting with your project supervisor to ensure that you come away with the information you need.

Supervisors are often required to indicate at the end of a project how much help they have provided, to try to make the playing field for assessment more even, but students receiving at least average help are likely to achieve better projects than those receiving very little, so do not stint on your contact with them for this reason.

Departments will have different rules and guidelines on what you can expect from a supervisor, but the typical balance of input you can expect might be something like that shown in the outline below.

Likely division of labour between student and supervisor for project

- *Choice of topic:* both input into this. The supervisor might suggest a fruitful area, but the student would then develop the detail, depending on their interest.
- *Literature search:* the supervisor would expect to make some initial suggestions and help if the student got stuck, but the student is expected to make the major contribution. This is likely to be ongoing during the project as different issues come up at each stage, and new material is published.

- *The research design and experimental detail* comes mainly from the student, but the supervisor would be expected to comment on feasibility. This is why it is very beneficial to have a supervisor who actually works in a relevant area.
- *Managing participants* is the responsibility of the student. A pilot will illustrate for you some of the difficulties that are likely to come up once the project moves off the drawing board.
- *Ethical approval:* you will need to check whether this is required, identify the correct forms, and establish who is expected to complete and submit these.
- *Running the project* is up to the student, unless there is an educational or clinical context where the supervisor's input may be required.
- *Data analysis:* proposals for this come from the student, but the supervisor would be expected to comment and offer some advice on interpreting the results after the student has carried out the analysis.
- *Feedback on a draft report:* this a tricky one as the supervisor is also normally one of the examiners, so universities often stipulate that feedback is only given on the first draft and never on the Discussion section. Check out the rules in your institution and plan accordingly.

5.4 Designing the project

Developing an answerable research question is an important and difficult first stage. The next stage is to design your research *protocol* (i.e. plan exactly what you are going to do to try to answer the question). Effectively, this means writing the first draft of the Methods section of your final project report.

Depending on the area under investigation, you will need to decide on most of the following.

- What participants will I be using? For example:
  - students
  - adults of a certain age range
  - children of a certain age group
  - certain categories of patients.
- Do I need a control group of a different kind of participant? For example:
  - children of a different age, or of the same age but a different level of achievement
  - patients from a different category to control for general effects of hospitalization
  - matched control group of the same age, etc.
- How will I be getting the information I need from them? For example:

- ○ questionnaire
- ○ standardized psychometric tests
- ○ structured interview
- ○ field observation
- ○ computerized testing
- ○ web-based testing.
- What will the experimental design be? For example:
  - ○ within group – the same participants tested, observed etc. in more than one condition – for example, comparing participants' cognitive abilities sober and after a drink
  - ○ between group – testing different groups of the same kind of participant in two situations – for example, comparing cognitive abilities of a group tested in the morning with the performance of a group tested in the afternoon; testing more than one kind of participant in the same situation – for example, comparing the cognitive abilities of men and women.
  - ○ **counterbalancing** order within groups to control, e.g., for practice effects.
- What equipment will be needed? For example:
  - ○ photocopied questionnaires
  - ○ standardized psychometric test sheets (do these need purchasing or can they be photocopied?)
  - ○ laptop
  - ○ laboratory equipment
  - ○ video or audio recording device.
- Where will I do the research and is suitable accommodation available? For example:
  - ○ school
  - ○ hospital
  - ○ room or laboratory in the department.
- What additional permissions will I need? For example:
  - ○ head and parents in a school
  - ○ Criminal Records Bureau registration (see page 168)
  - ○ ethical approval, including NHS ethical permission if the work is in a hospital (see page 144)
  - ○ owner – to work on private property.
- What additional information do I need to collect for my Methods section? For example:
  - ○ age and sex of participants
  - ○ details of equipment to be used – make and screen size of computers, video camera, etc.
  - ○ spatial arrangement of testing situation
  - ○ publishers of standardized tests to be used
  - ○ location of observational or other fieldwork.

- How will I analyse the results (and do I know how to do it)? For example:
  ○ comparing frequency data with chi square
  ○ comparing two groups with a t-test
  ○ calculating the correlation between two variables
  ○ using an analysis of variance (ANOVA) to see if two measures are affected differently by different conditions (see Figure 5.11)
  ○ using multiple regression techniques to see how much two or more different measures contribute to a particular outcome – for example, separating out the influence of class size and entry age on exam performance in schools.
- Cost:
  ○ am I going to incur costs such as travel, postage and printing, and how will they be met?

At this stage, the temptation is always to stick in a few more variables: 'I could look at the effects of **sex**, or age or hair colour, etc. as well as the variable I am really interested in.' It does no harm to collect information on things like this and you certainly should collect age and sex data to report in your Methods section. It is sometimes the case that you unexpectedly find when you are analysing the results that sex, age or hair colour are interesting variables. However, you should be careful about having too many variables in your design for two reasons: it may make it difficult to analyse effectively and it may mean testing more participants than you have access to or time for. Each new group you introduce will require sufficient participants to make the analysis possible. Our general advice is never to plan to do an ANOVA with more than three variables (factors) unless you are dating a statistician, and then you will probably not be able to understand their interpretation of the resulting interactions. So, if in doubt, keep it simple.

Tips: Starting to write early

➢ Don't worry if you don't know all the answers yet, or even all the questions – you can re-draft the report – but it's good to make a start while the deadline is still a long way off.

➢ The more drafts of your report you produce, the better it will be.

➢ Write out the main hypothesis at an early stage and agree it with your supervisor – you can always add additional ones when you see the results.

➢ When you have the hypothesis, you can start drafting the Introduction from the notes you have been taking while reading round the topic.

➢ Write a draft of the Methods section before you start the study. This will make clearer any operational decisions you need to take about how you are actually going to run the study. It will also identify the things you need to record to make the Methods section complete.

Quantitative versus qualitative research

One of the attractions of psychology is that it is a very heterogeneous subject with many different approaches and methodologies. None is definitively the correct one and most have something useful to offer. One of the apparently more significant distinctions is between quantitative and qualitative methodology. Quantitative methodology is where the researcher is essentially collecting numbers, either relating to some scale or order, or to the frequency with which events fall into different categories. Qualitative methodology, for example **action research**, is where the information collected is descriptive on the part of either the researcher or the participant. For example, the researcher may record their description of a piece of behaviour as it happens, or record the words of the participant as they answer relatively open-ended questions about their experiences in the area under investigation.

This distinction is certainly important but is not as dramatic or absolute as it is sometimes made out to be. You will find that staff are often firmly wedded to one or other approach in their own research and this may be linked to an ideological justification for their particular preference. A more pragmatic view is that both are actually difficult to do well and it is therefore better to specialize in one or the other. Certainly it is a myth, sometimes propagated among students, that **qualitative research** is easier than **quantitative research**. There is in fact a sophisticated methodology needed to draw effective conclusions from qualitative data. The underpinnings are in **grounded theory**, which is a formal methodology for deriving theory from data (which has a whole journal, the *Grounded Theory Review*, devoted to it), rather than, as in much research, using data to test a pre-ordained theory. Although the approach is not limited to qualitative data it is particularly suited to the first stage of the development of an understanding of human behaviour where the evidence is largely descriptive (see Figure 1.1). Descriptive data have to be analysed very carefully to avoid the researcher biasing the findings according to their prior views about what is going on (**experimenter bias**). **Discourse analysis** and **content analysis** provide systematic ways for doing this. There are now computer programs, for example NVivo, for helping with this kind of analysis, and the end product of such analyses may be numbers in the form, for example, of frequencies with which certain forms of discourse occur. So, even if you are doing a qualitative project, you may end up doing some statistics. It is beyond the scope of this book to describe these techniques in more detail, but your methodology course should cover them and will have recommended a suitable textbook. If not, and you want to do a qualitative project, then we would recommend Berg (2006), Banister et al. (1997), Charmaz (1995) or Smith (1995) as a starting point.

> **Tip: Horses for courses**
>
> ➤ If you are going to do a qualitative research project try to get a supervisor who is familiar with the methodology. (Similarly, of course, if you are doing a quantitative project, it is good to have a supervisor familiar with statistics.)

5.5 Getting ethical approval

It is a general rule that all research involving human participants in universities has to have obtained ethical approval before it can be started. This applies to everything from a first-year practical doing field observations through to large-scale research projects being run by a professor in your department. Obtaining approval means submitting an outline of what is going to be done to independent scrutiny. It serves three purposes.

1 Its main purpose is to protect the participants, and this is obviously particularly important if these are from a vulnerable group such as children or hospital patients.
2 As a secondary function, it protects the university by ensuring that nothing unethical is being done in its name.
3 It also protects the researcher as, provided they follow the procedure for which they have obtained approval, they will have the support of the university if things go wrong.

The formal process for obtaining approval will vary from institution to institution, but, unless your supervisor has already obtained generic approval for the kind of study you are doing, it will begin with you filling in a form. This will require a general account of what you are planning to do and answers to some specific questions about the nature of your participants, and so forth. Depending on the level of risk involved, it may be submitted to a committee, or one or two independent people, for scrutiny. It will then be returned to you with the outcome, which might be approval, approval subject to some amendments, or rejection.

The principles underlying decisions about research ethics are complex and much has been written about them (for example, Israel & Hay, 2006). The most useful source for psychologists is the policy document *Ethical Principles for*

Conducting Research with Human Participants published by the BPS and available on its website (www.bps.org.uk).

Your department may also have specific guidelines about such things as working with children or other vulnerable groups and, if in doubt, you should consult. There are, however, some general rules that you should be comply with if possible.

- Participants must give their **informed consent** to take part in the study. This has two parts:
  - an information sheet giving details of what the participant will experience and what will happen to the data that is being collected, an explicit statement that they may withdraw from the study at any time, advice that they may ask for the return of any information collected at any time, including after the study is finished, and contact details if they have any complaints or worries
  - a consent form for them to sign to say they have read and understood the information sheet and have had the opportunity to ask questions.
- Participants' anonymity must be preserved unless specific permission has been given not to do so. (Preserving anonymity means that no information should be released that would enable the participant to be identified – sometimes quite difficult in a **case study**.)
- There must be no coercion to take part in the study. (Coercion can take many forms, including financial reward and social pressure.)
- Deception must be kept to a minimum and should not be such that a reasonable person would be expected to object to it.
- Participants must be fully debriefed at the end of the experiment, particularly if there has been an element of deception.

Any exception to these rules – for example, the inability to obtain informed consent or to debrief, both of which are a particular problem with field studies – must be fully justified in an application and, as with coercion, must not involve any activities to which a reasonable person would object.

The more controversial the study the longer it is likely to take to get ethical approval, particularly if it has to go to a full university committee for consideration. It is also important to remember that any work done on NHS premises or involving NHS patients or staff requires NHS approval. This involves submitting an application through the national NHS system (NRES), which will be considered by a local health authority ethics committee (an LREC).

5.6 Running the project

By this stage, if your planning has been reasonably thorough and effective, running the project *should* follow a fairly pre-ordained path. Sometimes it does, but sometimes it does not.

The most common thing to go wrong is that you discover that your carefully planned experiment does not work because for some reason the participants do not behave in quite the way you expected or, particularly if you are doing fieldwork, are simply unavailable in the numbers or at the time you require. Participants may, for example, find the task too easy, or too difficult, or too unpleasant. Assuming you are able to collect some data, you have two choices: you can plough on and report the 'unexpected' finding; or you can treat the data you have collected so far as a pilot and modify your methodology. This is a moment to talk to your supervisor.

Another outcome that is seen by students as a problem, but that is not really one, is a negative result. You predict that X does Y, but you find it does not. This can certainly be disappointing: it is never nice to be proved wrong. However, in terms of advancing our knowledge it is as informative as a positive result. You have discovered that, in this situation, contrary to expectations, X does not do Y. That is just as interesting, may even be more interesting, than finding that X does do Y. So there is no need to be defensive when you come to write it up.

The other problems you are likely to encounter are more mundane: a shortage of participants, an equipment breakdown, a postal strike blocking the return of your questionnaires, and so on. These are sent to try you and you will have, in consultation with your supervisor, to overcome them as best you can. If they are really serious they should be written up as part of your report and they will be taken into account in deciding the final mark. The examiners will know all about the difficulties of doing research. Provided the problem was not because you started collecting data only a month before the hand-in date, but was genuinely outside your control and you took the initiative in trying your best to overcome the difficulty, then they will make generous allowance. Indeed, sometimes problems like these enable students to show enterprise and inventiveness that impress the examiners even more than if everything had run smoothly.

A good 'problem' to have is the possibility of doing a follow-up study: you run the research quickly and smoothly, and the preliminary results suggest a second study that could be run to answer a new but related question. This would be impressive if you are sure you have time, but beware of getting sucked in to something that will not leave you time to write up the study properly.

Finally, running the study will probably be an intermittent affair, with gaps caused by vacations or equipment breakdown. Use these gaps to work on the drafts of your Introduction and your Methods section. The Introduction will need fine-tuning after you have written your Results section and in order to articulate with the Discussion. However, the Methods section should be complete by the time you finish collecting data. The only exception might be the section on how you analysed your findings. If the analysis is at all complicated, it is common to put a sentence or two about it in the Methods, but they may need tweaking after you have actually done the analysis.

5.7 Reporting and analysing your results

This is the centrepiece of your project or dissertation and must be approached with thought and care. It is also the area where even very good students can go wrong. We are therefore devoting a substantial amount of time and space to it. So should you.

How to display psychological data effectively

You will by this time have written drafts of the Introduction and the Methods sections, and run the experiment. The most commonly required format for displaying data is the APA format, as with references, but check that this is the

Some advice from students on writing up projects
☑ My supervisor wasn't very sure of the best way to analyse my results, so I asked the guy who taught us statistics in the second year and he was incredibly helpful. ☑ A friend told me how to analyse my results, but he got it wrong. I wished I'd checked with my supervisor. ☑ I worked incredibly hard planning and running my project, and did it extremely well, but I didn't leave enough time for analysing and writing it up. So the report, which is the main thing the examiners look at, was, I know, not very good. I only got a 2:1 when I hoped to get a first. So leave more time than you can possibly imagine to fiddle around working out the best way to present and analyse your data, and then to proof-read what you have written very carefully.

case in your department. Generally, people are less fussy about following a particular style for figures and tables. The important thing is that they are well designed, accurate and clearly labelled, and the format is the same all the way through the report. It is worth giving some thought to this. The Results section is the centrepiece of your report and well-presented data will help to make it succinct, clear and professional in appearance. You should start by considering your data and thinking which method will present them to best effect.

Note: All the examples shown in this section are in APA format, but, as elsewhere, the data are invented to make the points more clearly.

Tables

Tables are an efficient way of presenting the exact numerical values, but most people find them quite difficult to interpret, so reserve them for your most important results. Table 5.1 offers an example in APA style.

Note: Tables are numbered separately from figures, and the legend appears at the top.

Table 5.1
Mean reaction times (RT) in ms and standard deviations (SD) of hockey and netball players performing motor tasks of varying difficulty

Level of difficulty	Hockey			Netball		
	RT	SD	N	RT	SD	N
Low	540	12.20	15	495	9.95	18
Moderate	790	18.73	15	787	23.28	12
High	1150	27.49	12	1240	34.20	15

Boxplots

Boxplots offer a very good way of visualizing the pattern of the data, showing more of their features than the alternatives. This does mean that they are complicated, take a little practice to interpret, and may not emphasize the particular feature you want to concentrate on in your report. For these reasons they may be used just for an initial exploration of the data before deciding to use a simpler line or bar chart in the Results section of your report. The best rule is to include a boxplot in your write-up only if there is no other way you can make the point you want to make. An example of this is shown in Figure 5.1.

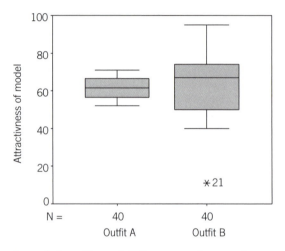

Figure 5.1. Boxplots of the effect of different outfits on the attractiveness of a model, rated out of 100.

The shaded areas show the middle 50% of the ratings, with the horizontal line in the middle of the shaded area indicating the value of the median rating. The top and bottom horizontal lines, at the end of each 'whisker', mark the highest and lowest ratings respectively. The numbers, 40 in this case, along the horizontal (X) axis record the number of participants in each group. The star marks a response by participant 21, which has been classified as an outlier and might be considered for exclusion from the data if justification for doing this can be found. (Maybe participant number 21 had previously seen this outfit on a celebrity she particularly disliked.)

This is the detail of how boxplots work, but you hardly need to know any of this to see that although the model is rated more or less the same in both outfits on average, the pattern of responses is very different. There is little variation between participants in the rating for the model when wearing Outfit A. Views on Outfit B are much more variable, with some people thinking the model looks considerably better or considerably worse than in Outfit A, while participant 21 rates her much lower than in Outfit A.

Tips: Using boxplots

➢ Use boxplots for an initial exploration of the data when you are comparing two or more groups.
➢ Thanks to the magic of **SPSS** they are very easy to generate, so it is worth having a look at boxplots of your data even if you do not include them in your write-up.

Line graphs

These are suitable for representing data that is a continuous variable – someone's weight, for example – so that readings can be made between the data collection points. Think carefully about the legend, which will establish the mindset of the person looking at the graph. Label both x (horizontal) and y (vertical) axes clearly and think about where each axis should start. As you will see in Experiment 2 (see page 157), it may be important to start the y axis at zero. Tiny effects can be

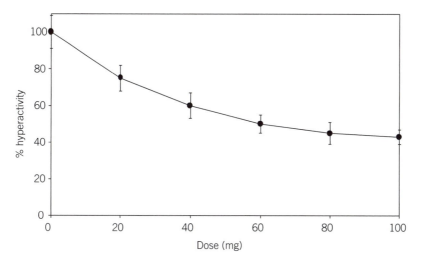

Figure 5.2. The effect of varying doses of the drug ZPC321 on the mean activity level of a group of hyperactive children measured as percentage of the activity level with a **placebo**; vertical lines show standard errors of the means.

made to look spuriously important by choice of scale. In fact, both Excel and SPSS are prone to do this for you automatically so that it is then surprising to find that the results are not significant. Andy Field (Field, 2005) should be consulted here. Some people are perfectionists about this and insist that you should always start the axes at zero. Others are less rigid and feel that it is more useful to spread the results so that they are more clearly displayed. Figure 5.2 shows a simple example of a line graph.

Bar charts

(Known as histograms when they are plotting frequencies.)

These are very useful for comparing the performance of several different **subjects**, or subject groups, across a number of different conditions, and can show a great deal of information very concisely. Figure 5.3 shows a relatively complex example.

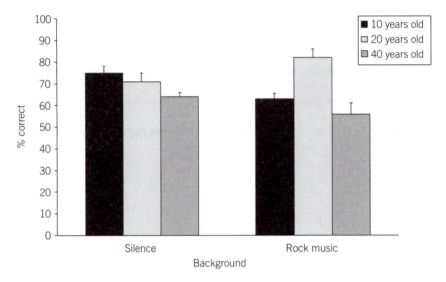

Figure 5.3. The mean performance of three age groups on a test of mental arithmetic with silence or loud rock music in the background; vertical lines show the standard errors of the means.

Interaction graphs

The data shown in Figure 5.3 could also be plotted as a line graph. This is shown in Figure 5.4.

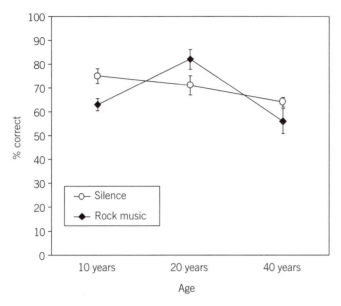

Figure 5.4. The mean performance of three age groups on a test of mental arithmetic with silence or loud rock music in the background; vertical lines show the standard errors of the means.

This is an example of an interaction graph: it shows the way two variables, age and background noise, interact with each other.

Error bars

Figures 5.3 and 5.4 both have vertical lines called error bars giving a measure of the amount of variation in the scores of individual participants around the group mean. Conventionally, error bars either show either the standard error, as here, or the 95% confidence interval (see Appendix 5).

Exercise 5.1 Deciding on the best way to show data

Figures 5.3 and 5.4 show exactly the same data in two different ways.

- Assuming the data are real (which they are not) what would you conclude about the effect of loud music on the ability to do mental arithmetic?
- Now decide which figure shows this conclusion most clearly.

See Appendix 2 for answer and comment.

Scatterplots

These are useful when you want to show the relationship between two variables. That is, when you want to decide whether one variable correlates with another. Each dot represents a single event or measurement rather than the mean of a set of measurements. Figure 5.5 shows the results of a hypothetical study investigating the relationship between the volume of noise and number of guests at a party.

If the points fall along a straight line (known as a trend line or regression line), as they do here, this implies a linear relationship and a high correlation between the two variables. The maximum correlation coefficient is 1. In this hypothetical case the correlation between the number of guests and the volume of noise is very high (0.98).

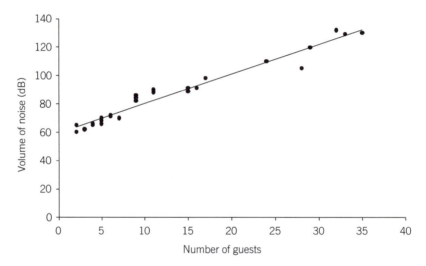

Figure 5.5. The relationship between the number of guests at a party and the volume of noise they make.

Tips: Displaying data effectively

➤ Number tables and figures separately.
➤ Place tables and figures as near to relevant material in the text as possible.
➤ All tables and figures should have clear legends so that they can be understood in a general sense without referring back to the relevant text, which may not be immediately adjacent.
➤ Always put a specific reference to each table or figure in the text.

Pie charts

These are not used all that commonly for representing psychological data, but there are circumstances where they are very valuable – for example, in representing the composition of a population where there are more than two or three components.

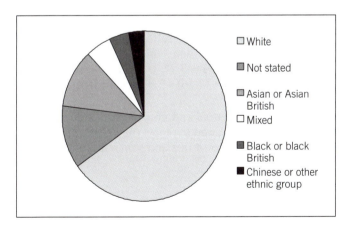

Figure 5.6. The ethnic mix of the town where the present study took place, as self-reported in the 2001 United Kingdom Census; ethnicity is classified according to the Level 1 Groups used in that census.

Figure 5.6 shows the ethnic composition of a medium-sized northern English town. Note that the slices are arranged in descending order, with the largest starting at 12 o'clock, which is how the APA likes them.

Reporting statistics

The best way of dealing with statistics in a report is to give a simple description of what statistical test you have used and why you have chosen it, before you go into the detailed outcomes. This can be in the Methods section, particularly if it is at all complicated, or when you come to it in the Results section. If you have used straightforward tests, like comparing means with a t-test or a simple ANOVA, then you can just report the results without explanation (see below for examples).

When you first write practical reports you may have been asked to begin the Results section with a description of your results in figures and tables (the descriptive statistics), followed by a separate account of your statistical analysis of the data (the **inferential statistics**).

When you are more practised, it is better to integrate the two. Report the result in tables and/or figures, then immediately below draw conclusions, supporting these with statistics. Imagine you are reporting the results of a two-part experiment that involved pre-test training followed by a memory test. You might include two figures (not shown here) for showing the results of each part, and write:

The performance of the three groups on the pre-test training is shown in Figure Y. They all performed equally well, $F(2, 16) = .10$, $p > .05$. Figure Z shows the results of the subsequent memory test. There was an overall effect of the training condition, $F(2, 16) = 5.23$, $p < .05$, and a post-hoc paired comparison showed that the results were in the predicted direction, with Group A performing better than both Group B, $t(16) = 1.85$, $p < .05$ (two-tailed), and Group C, $t(16) = 3.42$, $p < .01$ (two-tailed), and group B performing better than Group C, $t(16) = 2.01$, $p < .05$ (two-tailed).

If you do get significant differences and you want to indicate how large those differences are, then it is always good to report the effect size as well.

See Appendix 5 for a definition of this and some of the other common terms used in statistics.

Tip: Reporting statistical test results

➢   There are standard ways of reporting the results of statistical tests, which are designed to be clear and efficient – once you know the way they work. As with our figures and tables we have used the APA style.

5.8 Common errors of interpretation

Here are some errors we have seen in final-year projects. (Note that all the data are invented to illustrate the points clearly, so do not quote them as evidence!)

Experiment 1: The relation between body mass index (BMI) and seniority

The seniority of staff in a multinational company was ranked on a scale from 1–10 according to salary, and five employees were randomly selected from each point on the scale. Their weight and height was measured and the **body mass index (BMI)** (a measure of fatness, see Appendix 4) calculated. The results are shown in Figure 5.7.

Conclusion: 'There is a positive correlation between weight and seniority. Success makes you fat.' (Or should it be 'Being fat helps bring success'?)

What is wrong: There is a correlation between seniority and fatness, but this does not allow you to draw firm conclusions about one *causing* the other. In fact this is a classic case of a **tertium quid**. There is a third factor, age, which tends to bring both excess weight and seniority.

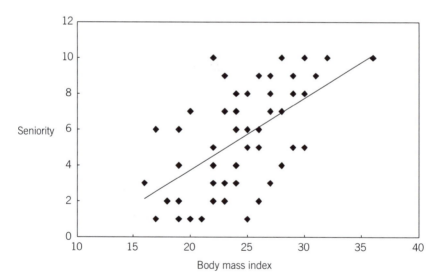

Figure 5.7. The relation between body mass index (BMI) and seniority in a multinational company; each point plotted represents an individual member of staff.

> ### Tip: Interpreting correlations
>
> ➤ A significant correlation between two variables just means that they vary together. It does not necessarily mean that one causes the other; although that may be the case.

Experiment 2: Sex and intelligence in psychology students

A total of 30 male and 30 female students were selected at random from the first-year class list of psychology students at a UK university. Their **IQs** were measured using the Borat Adult Intelligence Scale (BAIS). The results are shown in Figure 5.8.

Conclusion: 'In this cohort of students male students are more intelligent than female students.'

What is wrong: In fact, there was no significant difference between men and women ($t = 0.42$, $p > 0.05$, two-tailed). The bar chart is reproduced here as it was produced by Excel using that software's default settings. It has chosen a y axis

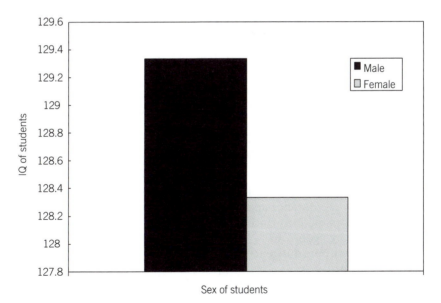

Figure 5.8. A comparison of the mean IQ scores of male and female psychology students at a UK university.

(vertical axis) that is quite inappropriate. The safe rule in situations like this is to start your y axis at zero. If you do this, and add some error bars, then it becomes obvious that there is no significant difference (see Figure 5.9). Even if the difference had been significant, it is tiny. This would be made much clearer by starting the y axis at zero. Reporting the effect size would also show this.

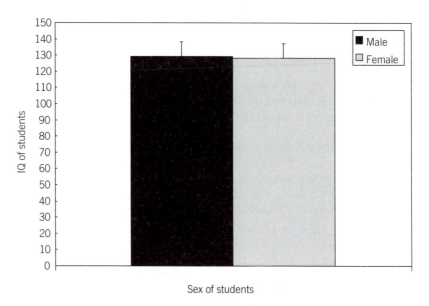

Figure 5.9. A comparison of the means and standard errors of IQ scores of male and female students at a UK university.

Experiment 3: Sex and motor skills in students

An opportunity sample of 20 male and 20 female students was recruited from the cafeteria. Their motor skills were assessed by rating their performance out of 100 on two tests: the distance and accuracy of throwing a ball, and the speed and accuracy of pressing a sequence of keys on a specially designed keyboard. The results are shown in Figure 5.10.

Conclusion: 'There is no difference in the motor skills of men and women in this sample of students.'

What is wrong: The basic conclusion is superficially correct, but it is misleading. By averaging over the two tasks, a very important difference between men and women has been lost. This difference becomes clear if the data are plotted in a different way (see Figure 5.11).

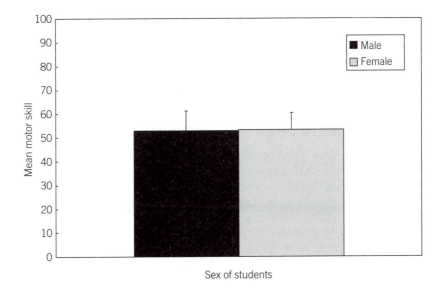

Figure 5.10. A comparison of the means and standard errors of the motor skills of male and female students at a UK university.

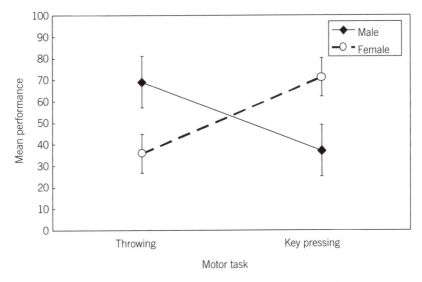

Figure 5.11. A comparison of the means and standard errors of the performance of male and female students at a UK university on two motor skill tasks.

Looking at this interaction graph, it is obvious that there may be a clear differ-ence between men and women: there is, in the jargon, an *interaction* between sex and the kind of motor skill, with men better at throwing and women better at the fine motor skill of systematic key pressing. This tentative conclusion should then be investigated with a two-factor (Throwing vs Key pressing) between-groups (Male vs Female) analysis of variance (ANOVA).

Experiment 4: The effect of alcohol on driving

Twenty volunteers were tested in a driving simulator on a test in which they had to drive their car through a narrow, complex route marked out by 40 traffic cones. The number of cones knocked over provided a measure of their driving skill. Their performance was measured twice, on different days, once after drinking a large glass of orange juice containing 50 ml of vodka (a standard double measure) and once after drinking plain orange juice. In order to counterbalance practice effects, ten participants were tested first after the alcoholic drink and ten were tested first after the non-alcoholic drink. The results are shown in Figure 5.12.

Conclusion: 'Although there is a small decrease in performance after alcohol, this is not significant ($t = 1.72$, $p > 0.05$, one-tailed). It is therefore safe to conclude that a double shot of alcohol has no effect on driving ability.'

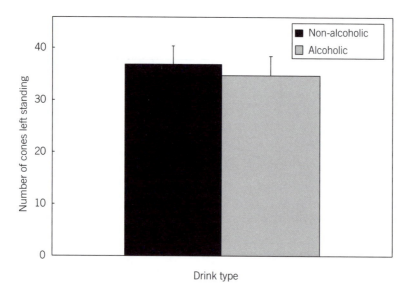

Figure 5.12. The effect of alcohol on driving skill, as measured by the number of traffic cones knocked over.

What is wrong: The graph is fine. The statistical analysis showing no difference is used correctly. The problem is that the test is too easy, so both groups are performing at or near 100% correct. There is therefore a *ceiling effect*, and this is almost certainly masking an alcohol-induced impairment. In fact, the t-test gives a probability of $p = 0.051$, which only just misses being significant. It would be worth reporting this actual value and concluding that although there is no difference between the conditions there is a trend in the direction of an impaired performance after alcohol. It would have been much better to have done a pilot study first to adjust the level of difficulty of the test so that, even after orange juice, some mistakes were being made, and taking care not to make the task so difficult that both participants were performing at chance in both conditions, creating a *floor effect*, which would also mask a genuine difference.

5.9 Writing up

The general structure of a research report should be very familiar to you by now, but check the section on 'Writing practical reports' (pages 113–114) carefully, running through the notes about the different sections of a research report.

The general aim is to write up your project as if you were preparing a manuscript for submitting it to a journal for publication. The only exception to this guide is that the figures and tables should be inset in the text, rather than grouped separately at the end as they would be for a journal submission.

Tip: Finding a model for your research report

> A good way to help to plan the final stretch of your writing is to find a recent journal article on a topic in the general area of your research that has been written in the style and format your department requires. Obviously, if this is APA, then take your model article from an APA journal. Your supervisor may be able to give you advice on this.

Rather than repeating the usual platitudes about writing concisely and in a relatively formal style, re-reading everything at least twice (once for sense, once for **typos**), and so on, that we have already been through in Chapter 4, we thought it would be helpful if we just gave you a checklist of things to tick off (Table 5.2). If possible, do this a day or two before the hand-in date so that you have time to correct any problems. This advice is based on long experience of the kind of errors or missed opportunities we have seen over the years in otherwise excellent project reports.

Is my title concise, elegant and informative?	
Does the Abstract contain details of the hypothesis, the method, the results and the conclusions?	
Does the Introduction lead clearly into the hypothesis to be tested?	
Does the Methods section contain enough detail for someone to repeat what I have done?	
Are the axes of all graphs labelled?	
Do the figures have error bars where appropriate?	
Do all tables and figures have legends?	
If the figures have error bars, do the legends say what these represent?	
Are all figures and tables mentioned at least once in the text?	
Are all the < and > symbols in my statistics reports the right way round?	
Does the Discussion refer back to points made in the Introduction?	
Are all references cited in the text in the References list?	
Are all references listed in the References section mentioned in the text?	
Are the references complete and correctly formatted?	
Are the appendices numbered and labelled?	
Is there a list of appendices at the start of the Appendix section?	
Are the pages numbered?	
Is the formatting of headings, etc. consistent throughout?	
Does the spell check on my word processor agree with my grammar and spelling?	

Figure 5.13. A checklist for ensuring your project report is in good order.

Finally . . . remember that "Genius is one per cent inspiration and ninety-nine per cent perspiration" (attributed to Thomas Edison, 1847–1931).

6

What next?

This chapter gives you a general introduction to the things you need to think about in considering a career. For more detailed and up-to-the-minute information on careers for psychology graduates, both within psychology and without, see our associated website: www.openup.co.uk/psychologysuccess.

You will see this icon again in the text that follows, to prompt you that there is more material about the topic on our website.

6.1 Introduction

Whether the career you choose lies in a formal branch of psychology or not, it will involve dealing with people, and you will find the insights you have gained during your psychology degree course invaluable. There is no doubt that one way to be successful is to think very carefully about how other people react to things, and we have included the TOMtips to draw your attention to some of the immediate, and sometimes ostensibly rather trivial, implications of things seen from someone else's point of view.

Assessing the potential of your degree

Bear in mind that there are plenty of successful people in senior jobs, whether psychologists or not, whose university careers were not particularly distinguished. Other factors start to count in the world of work, and being intelligent, imaginative, hard-working, reliable and professional (as opposed to popular) will take you a long way. If you really want to do something, you can probably find a way, but it may take you a bit more time and effort if you have underperformed on something along the way. The portfolio of skills you have been developing during your degree in psychology (look back at the QAA subject **benchmark** statement in Figure 2.11) will make you attractive to a wide range of employers. A combination of literacy and numeracy; an ability to evaluate evidence presented in the form of numerical data, good presentation skills and an understanding of teamwork, for example, should open all sorts of doors.

Compiling a good curriculum vitae

Where to start?

- You already have a great deal of useful material from your PDP file, so get it out and have a look at it.
- The university careers service (see page 168) will probably have software for designing a CV that you can use, and they will be able to advise you on what to include. It is worth spending time and effort on the presentation as this is the first thing anyone thinking of employing you or awarding you funding will see.

There is a solid factual background to any CV, which is simply a list of significant events in your life with dates. Make sure the facts are absolutely accurate and never be tempted to distort them. Dishonesty in a job application is a sackable offence. Keep this document stored safely on your computer and copy it before you edit it each time you use it, so that you can always go back to this backbone every time you have to make an application. In our experience, CVs are often required in a hurry, so it pays to keep them up to date.

Tips: Providing the right information

➤ Do not forget that information on social networking websites, like Facebook, MySpace and Bebo, is effectively public knowledge, and many employers are now regularly logging on to them to vet job applicants.
➤ We both keep a box labelled 'Things I have done' and throw records of all kinds – agendas, programmes, letters of thanks and invitations – in to it. It is extremely useful when you cannot quite remember the title of the

training you attended, the name of the conference at which you gave a **paper**, the details of some group to whom you gave a talk, the exact date that something happened, or even the fact that once upon a time you got a certificate that states you can skate backwards. You never know!

Please see our website for further help with this, including an exercise on presenting your details in ways that echo the job description, emphasizing the relevance of your experience to the post.

Finding suitable referees

The problem in the early stages is to find a range of referees, rather than just people who know you as an undergraduate. Probably the ideal referees for a first post would be your university tutor (or someone else in the psychology department with whom you have had a particular working relationship, such as your project/dissertation supervisor) and someone from a work context, either a placement during your course or a relevant post you have held pre-university or during the vacation. The more recent the contact you have had with them the better, assuming that you have matured and developed during your degree!

There is more help available on this on our website.

TOMtip

❖ Do remember that lecturers have to write many references each year, so the more you can do to help them, the more detailed and appreciative the reference is likely to be.

Interviews

Psychological research demonstrates over and over again that interviews are not a good way of predicting how someone will function in a role, and yet employers persist in using them for selection.

Our website describes the interview process and gives you some useful advice on how to handle it.

Networking

Networking probably plays a greater role in career development than is usually recognized. Some people are naturally better at this than others, but with a little thought and planning, you can develop and maintain a range of people you have come across on whom you can rely for information, help, advice and specific contacts. One rule here is to think about what they are going to get from their contact with you (you will recognize a TOMtip here). If you offer to look something up or email a piece of information for them, do it. They will hopefully remember this when you ask a favour in return.

The happenstance of information about a vacancy not on your usual information channels, or some unusual source for a travel grant, might just give you an opening. While you are on the course, take the time to chat to other students in the department and pick up what you can glean from the grapevine. Administrative staff (if they can spare the time) are wonderful sources of current information. Electronic mail lists in particular areas of interest, particularly the BPS one, are worth joining, and use search engines to comb through the web with very carefully selected keywords. Make the most of any conference opportunities, particularly if you can give a poster or ask intelligent questions.

6.2 Ideas about careers in general

Getting experience through placements

If you are not sure where you are heading, start by looking at your personal development profile and consider what it indicates to you about what you find interesting and enjoy doing. It may at once be apparent that you are very lacking in experience in areas you may be contemplating as a career, and this is the moment to use any projects or placements built into the course to explore these, supplementing them with other vacation work where possible. It is also now an increasingly common practice, particularly for those wishing to get on to a clinical psychology course, to organize a placement or work experience after graduation. If nothing else, it will help you decide if you have made the right decision about a possible career. It can be difficult to organize and you may have to use personal contacts to find somewhere to take you on, but it can be very worthwhile.

What do psychology graduates do?

Figure 6.1 shows an analysis of what psychology graduates do immediately after graduation, taken from the Prospects website (http://www.prospects.co.uk)

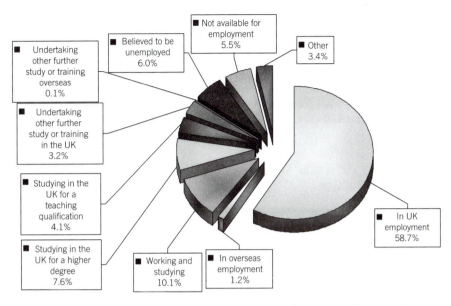

Figure 6.1. The first employment destination of psychology graduates. (Source of raw data: HESA Destinations of leavers from Higher Education 2005/6).

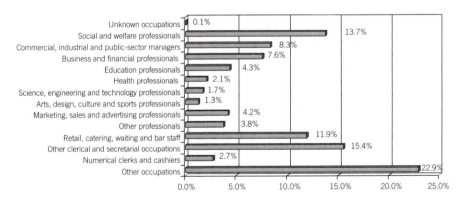

Figure 6.2. Further analysis of 'UK employment' segment in Figure 6.1, showing different employment areas.

You will see from the pie chart in Figure 6.1 that 25.1% of psychology graduates are involved in some kind of further study or training. Your degree is often only the first step on a professional path.

Using the university careers service

The university careers service should be the obvious first port of call when you are starting to consider a career but many students leave this very late, until they are distracted by preparing for final-year exams. It makes good sense to make contact with the careers service at least by the end of your second year and respond to any contact they make with you. They have vast experience and a range of services to offer; for further details, see our website.

Other sources of advice

Your department will also be a useful source of information and advice. Your tutor and other members of staff will be a particularly useful source of advice if they have interests in the area you wish to investigate. For more on sources of help from the department see our website.

Tips: Careers sessions

➤ If there is no session offered on different careers, ask one of the student reps if they can suggest the need for one at the next staff–student meeting.
➤ If all else fails, you could try organizing one with a group of friends and the help of a lecturer in suggesting whom to ask.

A good class of degree is very helpful for this next move in your life. Indeed it is a prerequisite for many areas of postgraduate training in psychology, but it is only a gate into the next stage. If you want to become a practising psychologist and you have not got, or are unlikely to get, at least a 2:1, do not despair, the British Psychological Society website (www.bps.org.uk/careers) gives careful and detailed advice on how to overcome this for each specialist branch of psychology.

Criminal Records Bureau

You should be aware that anyone intending to work in a school or any setting where they will have 'substantial unsupervised access' to children or vulnerable adults has to register with the Criminal Records Bureau (CRB), which checks police records and, where relevant, information held by the Department of Health (DH) and the Department for Children, Schools and Families (DCSF).

There are two levels of CRB check, Standard and Enhanced Disclosure, and the level required will depend on where you are proposing to work.

For more detailed information go to the CRB website (www.crb.gov.uk) and our website.

6.3 Regulation

The Role of the British Psychological Society and the Health Professions Council

The British Psychological Society (BPS) was established in 1901 as a professional society to share specialist knowledge and information. It has now grown to 45,000 members and, as the number of areas within psychology has multiplied, specialist Divisions, Sections and Groups have been set up to facilitate a more focused exchange in particular areas of psychology. They all have links within the main BPS website (www.bps.org.uk) and if you are wondering whether to aim for one of these, it makes sense to follow the link and have a look at the sorts of things going on there.

The BPS also currently regulates many of the professional strands in psychology through the following two particular formal requirements.

Graduate Basis for Registration (GBR)

This acts as an initial gateway controlling those who enter the profession. If you have a BPS-accredited honours degree at class 2.2 or better you will automatically achieve Graduate Basis for Registration, and you should check that the course you are on has this accreditation. One point to watch out for, particularly if you are doing combined honours or following a major/minor structure in a modular system, is that you take sufficient psychology modules to give you GBR.

Chartered Psychologist

The number of people calling themselves psychologists and offering psycho-logical services is on the increase, and some have no recognized qualifications and are not answerable to any recognized professional body, so registration was introduced to provide a mechanism of quality control and give clients some professional safeguard. The British Psychological Society was authorized to set up and run the Register of Chartered Psychologists to protect the public, and the title

'Chartered Psychologist' is legally recognized. To achieve Chartered status, individuals must have:

- an accredited first degree in psychology giving GBR
- a recognized postgraduate qualification, *or* undergone approved postgraduate training and supervision
- been judged 'fit to practise' independently
- agreed to follow a strict code of conduct and be answerable to a disciplinary system, in which non-psychologists form the majority.

Registration is not currently a legal requirement to work as a psychologist as things stand, but employers tend to prefer to appoint people with Chartered status as it gives some guarantee about qualifications and professional standards. *The Directory of Chartered Psychologists*, listing all those who have achieved this, can be found in main public libraries and is available on the BPS website.

The BPS also monitors the continuing professional development (CPD) of practising psychologists, which ensures that they remain up to date with current practice.

At the postgraduate level, these regulatory functions will be taken over by the Health Professions Council (HPC) sometime during 2009, so watch our website for more details on regulation and continual updates on the state of play as this switch is effected. At the time of writing the government's draft legislation is proposing to register seven specialist areas of psychology: clinical, counselling, educational, forensic, health, occupational, and sport and exercise, and two generic titles 'Registered Psychologist' and 'Practising Psychologist'.

In each case it is the title that would be protected. So it will become illegal for someone to call themselves by one of these nine titles unless they have followed the appropriate training course accredited by the HPC and have subsequently kept up to date in their area by undertaking regular continuous professional development (CPD) (see page 176).

6.4 Careers in psychology

There are many career strands in psychology and we discuss the major ones, listed below, on our website with up-to-date information on contacts for the next step, training, funding and employment opportunities.

- Academic: becoming a university lecturer
- Business psychology
- Clinical psychology
- Coaching psychology
- Counselling psychology
- Educational psychology
- Forensic psychology
- Graduate mental health worker
- Health psychology
- Neuropsychology
- Occupational psychology
- Psychotherapy
- Sport and exercise psychology
- Teaching psychology in schools and colleges

The BPS has a very detailed and helpful summary of different career options in psychology, giving qualification routes, a description of where they work and who they work with, relevant experience, remuneration details, where jobs are advertised, and advice for mature students, those with 2:2s and those from overseas, which we suggest you consult (www.bps.org.uk/careers). It also publishes a valuable regular section on careers in its monthly magazine for members, The Psychologist.The Divisions, Sections and Special Groups of the BPS are obvious sources of focused information and can be accessed through the main website, but for an introduction see the website associated with this book. If you take out student membership of the BPS this will give you access to its quarterly magazine, *Psych-Talk* (www.bps.org.uk/smg), which covers the kinds of issues that will be concerning you. It could also be helpful to look at the graduate prospects website (www.prospects.ac.uk), and the Higher Education Psychology network (www.psychology.heacademy.ac.uk) is collecting case studies of careers from psychology graduates.

6.5 Postgraduate courses

These usually assume applicants will have GBR status, whatever route has been taken to acquire it, although it may not be compulsory for some academic or more general interest courses.

Accredited professional training in psychology

GBR will be compulsory for any course accredited by the BPS or the HPC for professional training. If an applied postgraduate course does not appear to require it, check carefully that it is recognized in the field and does nevertheless lead to job opportunities. The standard pattern leading to BPS Chartered Psychologist status is described above (page 169). Currently the areas in which there is accredited postgraduate training leading to Chartered status are: clinical, counselling, educational, forensic, health, occupational, sport and exercise, and teaching and research. These areas of psychology have carefully mapped, detailed progression routes leading to Chartered status and you should read the specialist sections on our website.

Although it is very likely that graduates wishing to continue their career in an area of psychology will need to take a further relevant qualification, this could be straight after graduating, after some relevant practical experience, or sometimes in mid-career as continuing professional development. If it is possible, it will probably pay you in the long run to take the route through formal qualifications even if you manage initially to obtain a post without them. The world in general is moving towards a culture that relies on formal qualifications, and you do not want to be caught out some years hence because you have not got the right piece of paper!

Training for other careers in psychology

It is likely that students wishing to continue their career in an area of psychology that does not yet have an accredited route will also need to take a further relevant qualification. You can get an idea of what is available more widely by going onto the graduate prospects website (http://www.prospects.ac.uk), which as we write has 688 postgraduate courses suitable for psychology graduates, ranging from postgraduate certificate (PGCert), postgraduate diploma (PGDip), master of arts (MA), master of science (MSc) and master of philosophy (MPhil), to taught doctor of philosophy (PhD) (often known as professional doctorates). These are all help-fully summarized by region.

This whole range of other specialist areas open to graduate psychologists for which there is not yet an accredited training route (although some of them might form part of the training in broader areas of applied psychology) includes: animal psychology, art therapy, aviation psychology, behaviour analyst, **cognitive behavioural therapy**, cognitive psychology, consumer psychology, developmental psychology, evolutionary psychology, gambling psychology, humanistic psychology, hypnotherapy, investigative psychology, music therapy, organizational psychology, parapsychology, political psychology, **psychoanalysis**, psycho-oncology, psychosomatics and social psychology.

Embarking on a PhD

The route to a research-based PhD is very often through a taught Master's pro-gramme with particular input on research methods – in other words, a 1+3 model. The taught year is sometimes known as an MRes (master in research) or may have a more specific title with more focused content. All PhD students are then regis-tered initially for an MPhil, converting to PhD registration only when they have won their spurs and reached a certain stage in their project, usually at some point in the second year. Funding is a major issue for postgraduate work and you should explore what possibilities are available. Find out what previous awards have been made in your chosen area in the department of your choice and be prepared to spend time and effort looking for less obvious sources. See our associated website for information on becoming a university lecturer and suggestions on funding for a PhD.

Other related postgraduate courses

There are also courses open to people with psychology degrees leading into dif-ferent related fields such as addictive behaviours, audiology, counselling and criminology.

6.6 Working and training abroad

Europe

The European Federation of Psychologists' Associations (EFPA) (www.efpa.be) provides a forum for European co-operation in academic training, psychological practice and research. There are 32 member associations representing about 180,000 psychologists. EFPA is concerned with promoting and improving psychology as a profession and as an academic discipline, and the member associations include practitioners as well as academic psychologists.

EuroPsy

This was established in 2005 in response to Directive 2005/36/EC following the Bologna declaration to promote European mobility, and denotes a European standard equivalent to BPS Chartered Psychologist status (i.e. three-year undergraduate degree, two-year postgraduate degree and one-year supervised practice). It enables individual psychologists to be recognized across the 32 national member associations in the European Federation of Psychologist Associations and is currently being trialled in six countries including the UK. Applicants can download the form from www.bps.org.uk/europsy and more information is available at www.efpa.be. Successful registration confers the title Registered EuroPsy Psychologist.

There is also currently a mutual recognition agreement between the UK and Republic of Ireland, and undergraduate degrees are recognized as the basis for postgraduate training in either country.

The USA

There are two national organizations for psychologists, as discussed below.

1 The American Psychological Association (APA) is a 'scientific and professional organization' with 148,000 members and 53 professional divisions, and is the American equivalent of the BPS. Its website (www.apa.org) has a section, 'PsyCareers', which covers careers both within psychology and without, and a large range of other information.
2 The Association for Psychological Science (APS) (www.psychological science.org) was founded in 1988 and has about 18,000 members. Its mission is 'to promote, protect, and advance the interests of scientifically oriented psychology in research, application, teaching, and the improvement of human

welfare'. It runs four **journals** and has subsections with information on research, journals and books, and jobs in psychology.

Rest of the world

For the addresses of the other main psychological associations across the world see our associated website.

6.7 Other careers

The value of your skills

Many employers are very vague about psychology and have a foggy concept of something that lies somewhere between astrology and psychiatry, so you will need to be very clear about the transferable skills you have acquired from your psychology degree. Use the QAA benchmarking statement (see Figure 2.11) to set out your stall illustrating what you can offer, and populate it from your PDP material. Applicants are usually very anxious to describe what they have done in an application, but not always so good at expressing it in terms of the job description from the employer. It pays to look very carefully at this and try to view your life so far in terms of their criteria. It is amazing how things you had not really seen the relevance of can come into focus.

Becoming an entrepreneur

There is a great deal of emphasis, following the Lambert Review in 2003 (www.hm-treasury.gov.uk/consultations_and_legislation/lambert/consult_lambert_index.cfm), on supporting the development of academic staff and students as entrepreneurs, and encouraging them to set up small businesses with various forms of training and support. There will be staff in the university with the specific remit to assist student entrepreneurs, and if you are considering this you should certainly go and talk to them about the possibilities. Most universities have science parks or business parks that provide a hothouse environment for such developments. Funding in the early stages is likely to be a real issue (watch *Dragons' Den (www.bbc.co.uk/dragonsden)* for an illustration of some of the pitfalls), so you will not be surprised if we urge caution.

6.8 Longer term

Continuing professional development logs

The pace of advance, particularly in a subject like psychology, is very rapid, and in order to keep abreast of your profession you are going to need constant updating, known as continuing professional development, or CPD (http://www.bps.org.uk/professional-development/cpd/cpd_index.cfm). With the introduction of statutory regulation through the Health Professions Council, the requirement for a CPD summary log of a minimum of 40 hours' CPD activity every year is likely to become compulsory for those with practising certificates (see our associated website for the latest information).

Logs can currently be submitted online using the BPS Online Planning and Recording System (www.bps.org.uk/cpd-word-summary-log). The log is due for submission three months before the date for renewal of the practising certificate). If you have followed the PDP formats earlier in the book (see pages 57–62) you will be well practised in the recording, reviewing and reflecting required.

Lifelong learning

You are likely to require updating not only in your specialist field but in other areas that touch upon your work, such as information technology, ethics and government policy. Our mental model for this is one of a climbing frame, where you may need to climb sideways or even down a level to acquire skills that have become relevant (information technology is an obvious example for older learners), as opposed to climbing the professional ladder in psychology where expertise and knowledge and qualifications are built rung upon rung.

Appendix 1 How to reference your work

It is standard academic practice to acknowledge the source of the ideas and information that you have used in writing your assignment. While it is expected that you will use the ideas, data and writings of others to support your own work, it is important that you acknowledge that they come from somewhere else, and the reference is designed to provide an accurate, detailed and stylized guide that should enable someone else to find the source.

A citation and reference are required when you:

- quote another person word for word, regardless of whether it is a phrase, sentence or paragraph
- paraphrase, summarize, or refer to ideas or data from someone else
- incorporate tables, figures or diagrams from another source.

You should distinguish between a citation and a **reference** as follows.

- *Citations* are used to refer to the source of a particular idea or piece of information in the text of your essay, and simply consist of the name of the author and the year of publication. If it is a verbatim quotation you should also give the page number.
- *References* to all the authors mentioned in the text are then collected alphabetically at the end, giving full bibliographic details including title, author source, edition, page numbers, place of publication and publisher, according to a particular format prescribed by the reference system being used. Only references cited in the text should appear in the reference list.

There are several referencing systems in common use, such as Harvard, the American Psychological Association (APA), Oxford, and the Museums and Libraries Association (MLA). Historically, and in arts subjects, it is common to have references as a footnote at the bottom of the relevant page, but now, particularly in science, the convention is to group them at the end, as described above. The system in most common use for psychology is the APA, as laid out in its *Publications Manual* (APA, 2001), which is used by the BPS as well. So we have used it in this book to familiarize you with it. However, you should find out what is standard in your psychology department at the beginning and use it right from the start, always making your own notes of references in the correct format. This will:

- stop you from getting confused
- save you a great deal of hassle when you are under pressure to hand in an assignment on time.

So here are some examples. Note particularly the hanging indent (i.e. after the first line, everything is inset by about 1 cm – in Word, use *Format* → *Paragraph* → *Special* to do this), and all the full stops and commas.

Referencing journal articles

In the text

Just give surnames and year of publication:

Latto and Latto (2008) reported that . . .

or

It has been reported (Latto & Latto, 2008) . . .

Note the use of the '&' in the bracketed citation, but not in the text.

In the reference section

Include the following (so you need to record all these when you are making notes on an article): author's last name, initials, year of publication in parentheses, title of article, title of journal in italics, volume, issue number and page numbers of the article. For example:

Latto, R., & Campion, J. (1986). Approaches to consciousness: psychophysics or philosophy? *Behavioral and Brain Sciences, 9*(1), 36–37.

Note that the APA convention is not to include the issue number, (1) in this case. This is annoying because it can be helpful in finding a reference and we usually try to include it if we know it as we have done both here and in the reference section of this book. It would be a remarkably pedantic tutor who did not think this was a good idea as well.

Referencing books

The format for referencing a book is the same in the text as for journals. In the reference section record: author's last name, author's initials, year of publication in parentheses, title of book in italics, place of publication and name of publisher. For example:

Latto, J., & Latto, R. (2009). *Study skills for psychology students*. Maidenhead, England: McGraw-Hill/Open University Press.

Referencing specific chapters in edited books

The format for referencing a chapter in the References section is: author's last name, author's initials, year of publication in parentheses, title of chapter, name of editor(s), the editor(s) abbreviation in parentheses, title of book, page numbers, place of publication and name of publisher. For example:

Latto, R. (1995) The brain of the beholder. In R. Gregory, J. Harris, P. Heard, & D. Rose (Eds.), *The artful eye* (pp. 66–94). Oxford, England: Oxford University Press.

Referencing work from a secondary source

This is the thing that seems to give students most trouble, but the principle is quite logical. In the text, name the original work and the secondary source:

Lea (1999, as cited in Latto & Latto, 2009)

Then in the References section just list the primary source:

Latto, J., & Latto, R. (2009). *Study skills for psychology students*. Maidenhead, England: McGraw-Hill/Open University Press.

Referencing newspaper/magazine articles

Where there is no identifiable author, as is common in newspapers, newsletters and magazines, in the References section lead with the title of the article, give a precise date of publication in parentheses, the title of the publication, and page numbers:

Caffeine linked to mental illness in new British study. (1991, July 13). *New York Times*, pp. 13–15.

In the text, give the title and year, abbreviating the title if it is long:

There has been a recent newspaper report of an association between high caffeine intake and depression (Caffeine linked to mental illness, 1991).

Referencing internet sources

If you have retrieved a journal article or book that was originally published in hard copy, then give the reference to that in the normal way, as shown above. Otherwise you always need to give the web address (URL) and the date retrieved. Websites vary enormously and you may need to consult the APA *Publications Manual*.

In the text

If you have the author's name and date use these as in standard citations (see above).

In cases where there is no identifiable author, give the title of the document/article and the date:

Children under 5 are most at risk of contracting the disease (New Child Vaccine, 2001).

If there is no identifiable date, you should use the n.d. (no date) notation.

When citing an entire website, give the address of the site:

Kidspsych is a wonderful interactive website for children (http://www.kidspsych.org).

In general, the first part of the citation should also be the first part of the entry in the References section so that it can be found easily.

In the reference section

The required information for referencing internet media is the following: author's last name, author's initials, year of document creation (if available), title of work, date retrieved and URL. For example:

Campbell, D.P. (1999) Visual illusory effectation. Retrieved March 27, 2000, from
http://www.sight.com/illusion.html

Note that no full stop is used after a URL.
    When there is no author for a web page, the title moves to the first position of the reference entry:

New child vaccine (2001) Retrieved March 21, 2001, from http://news.ninemsn.
com.au/health/story_13178.asp

If there is no identifiable date, you should use the n.d. (no date) notation.

Digital object identifier (DOI)

As websites tend to be ephemeral, a new convention called the **digital object identifier (DOI)** has been introduced. This is a permanent identifying number given to an electronic document unrelated to its current location, so a scientific paper or article can be located through this permalink. When a DOI is available, include the DOI instead of the URL in the reference. Publishers who follow best practice will publish the DOI prominently on the first page of an article. Because the DOI string can be long, it is safest to copy and paste whenever possible.

In conclusion

This may all seem very pernickety and tiresome, but we can assure you that when you have spent a frustrating hour trying to find something in the library or searching electronically, only to find that your reference was a dud, you will appreciate that this is one place where absolute accuracy really pays off.

Exercise A.1 When is a reference required?

	Yes	No
1 When you quote exactly what someone said in speech marks		
2 When you draw on information from another specific source		
3 When describing a theory originated by someone else		
4 When you include tables, figures or diagrams from another publication in your assignment		
5 When you incorporate data from another study		
6 When you identify original references that you have not read (secondary sources) from something you have actually read (primary source)		
7 When you collect together material from a number of sources and paraphrase it		
8 When you copy and paste items from websites		
9 When you want to refer to something you saw in a newspaper		
10 When you use material from a textbook		
11 When summarizing facts that are part of general knowledge		

See Appendix 2 for the answer.

Quotations

Short quotations, of fewer than 40 words, should be enclosed in double quotation marks and incorporated in the text. For example:

Nijstad, Stroebe and Lodewijkx (2006) conclude that "people produce more ideas when working alone as compared to when working in a group" (p. 31).

Longer quotations, of 40 words or more, should be started on a new line and indented by about 1.25 cm. For example:

In summarizing the literature on group productivity, Nijstad, Stroebe and Lodewijkx (2006) conclude that:

> Almost 50 years of brainstorming research has consistently shown that, when it comes to productivity, idea generation might best be left to individuals instead of groups: *N* individuals who work alone and whose non-overlapping ideas are pooled . . . produce more and better ideas than *N* individuals who work in an interactive group. (p. 31)

Quotations should be completely accurate, with any omissions in the middle indicated with spaced full stops (ellipsis) as in the example. You should also always give the page number if possible so that the reader can find the quotation easily in the original source. The one exception is with quotations from the web where there is no page number, but here the reader can use an electronic search to find the quotation in the original.

Appendix 2 Answers to exercises

Exercise 2.5: Neglecting base rates

Correct answer

There is a 47.6% (i.e. roughly 1 in 2) chance that her baby will have Down's syndrome.

Results of a survey among professionals and patients

Overall, most responses (86%) were incorrect. Obstetricians gave significantly more correct answers (although still only 34%) than either midwives (0%) or pregnant women (9%). Many health professionals were confident in their incorrect responses.

An explanation of how to derive the correct answer by taking the base rate into account

- If 10,000 pregnant women were tested, we would expect 100 (1% of 10,000) to have babies with Down's syndrome.
- Of these 100 babies with Down's syndrome, the test result would be positive for 90 (90% of 100) and negative for 10.
- Of the 9900 unaffected babies, 99 (1% of 9900) will also test positive, and 9801 will have a negative test result.
- So, out of the 10,000 pregnant women tested, we would expect to see 189 (90+99) positive test results. Only 90 of these actually have babies with Down's syndrome, which is 47.6%.
- Therefore, 47.6% of pregnant women who have a positive result to the test would actually have a baby with Down's syndrome.

Exercise 5.1 Deciding on the best way to show data

The general conclusion is that, without background music, the performance of people deteriorates with age, at least from 10 years old onwards, but that different age groups are affected in different ways by loud music. The performance of 10 and 40 year olds is impaired, while 20 year olds show an improvement.

Both figures show this, and which you find clearer is to some extent a personal preference, but we prefer the interaction graph (Figure 5.4).

Exercise A.1 When is a reference required?

This exercise was designed to help you learn the principles of referencing, and to illustrate where the answers shade from black and white to grey. Only question 11 requires the answer no. In all the other situations you should aim to produce a reference, even if it is only a secondary one. The general rule is that you should always give a reference if you possibly can.

Appendix 3 Acronyms and abbreviations

Terms in bold are defined in the Glossary (Appendix 4).
Terms in italic are from statistics and are defined in Appendix 5.

AGR	Association of Graduate Recruiters
aka	also known as
ANOVA	*Analysis of Variance*
APA	American Psychological Association
BBSRC	Biotechnology and Biological Research Council
BMI	**Body Mass Index**
BPS	British Psychological Society
CBT	**Cognitive Behavioural Therapy**
CER	Conditioned Emotional Response
CIT	Computing and Information Technology
CPD	Continuing Professional Development
CR	Conditioned Response
CRB	Criminal Records Bureau
CS	Conditioned Stimulus
DCSF	Department for Children, Schools and Families
DIUS	Department for Innovation, Universities and Skills
DOI	**Digital Object Identifier**
ECDL	**European Computer Driving Licence**
EEG	Electroencephalography
EPR	Experiment Participation Requirement
EPS	Experimental Psychology Society
EPSRC	Engineering and Physical Sciences Research Council
ESRC	Economic and Social Research Council
fMRI	functional Magnetic Resonance Imaging
GBR	**Graduate Basis for Registration**
HEI	Higher Education Institution
HPC	Health Professions Council
ICT	Information and Communications Technology
IQ	**Intelligence Quotient**
IT	Information Technology

LGN	Lateral Geniculate Nucleus
LRC	Learning Resource Centre
LREC	Local Research Ethics Committee (of the NHS)
MCQ	Multiple-Choice Question
MCT	Multiple-Choice Test
MRC	Medical Research Council
MRI	Magnetic Resonance Imaging
NHS	National Health Service
NRES	National Research Ethics Service (of the NHS)
OFFA	Office for Fair Access (to higher education)
PBL	Problem-Based Learning
PC	Personal Computer
PDP	Personal Development Profiling (or Planning)
PVC	Pro Vice-Chancellor
QAA	Quality Assurance Agency for Higher Education
q.v.	**quod vide**
REM	**Rapid Eye Movement** phase in sleep
SD	*Standard Deviation*
SDT	**Signal Detection Theory** (aka Signal Decision Theory)
SE	*Standard Error*
SEQ	Student Evaluation Questionnaire (your chance for revenge)
SLC	Student Loans Company
SPSS	**Statistical Package for the Social Sciences**
SWOT	Strengths, Weaknesses, Opportunities, Threats
TMS	Transcranial Magnetic Stimulation
ToM	**Theory of Mind**
UCAS	Universities and Colleges Admissions Service
UCR	Unconditioned Response
UCS	Unconditioned Stimulus
URL	**Uniform Resource Locator**
USB	Universal Serial Bus (a standard for interfacing peripheral devices)
VC	Vice-Chancellor
VLE	Virtual Learning Environment
WoK	**Web of Knowledge**
www	**world wide web**

Appendix 4 Glossary

(See also Appendix 5 Common terms (and some of their alternatives) used in statistics.)

For more information, try also looking up a word in the index, especially if it is not included here.

Words in bold have their own definition.

Acronym	A real, or at least pronounceable, word made up from the initial letters of a phrase or list; they can provide a useful **mnemonic** (see *Big Five* and **SWOT analysis** for examples)
Action research	A reflective and iterative process of diagnosis, planning and review to solve problems and improve professional practice
Amnesia	Loss of memory; see **Retrograde amnesia** and **Anterograde amnesia**
Anterograde amnesia	**Amnesia** for new events occurring after the trauma – a head injury, for example – that caused the amnesia
Anthropomorphism	The attribution of human characteristics and qualities to non-human beings or inanimate objects
Autism	A developmental disorder characterized by severe impairments in social interactions and language, resulting in restricted interests, repetitive behaviour and an obsessive desire for sameness
Base rate neglect	The tendency we all have to make judgements about the likelihood (probability) of something happening without taking into account the prior odds (base rate) of that thing happening; one of the main reasons why we need statistics to help us evaluate information (see the examples in the section an 'Experimental design and statistics' (pages 44–48); also known as the base rate fallacy
Benchmark	A standard against which you measure or compare something

Bias	See **Demand characteristics, Experimenter bias, Halo effect, Observer bias** and **Signal detection theory**
Bibliographic software	Software for storing, grouping and searching reference lists; will usually have a facility for citing while you write (cwyw), which allows you to call up a reference to put in what you are writing and to create a reference list at the end
Big Five (Five Factor model)	The five factors of personality identified empirically by Goldberg (1993): Openness to experience, Conscientiousness, Extraversion, Agreeableness and Neuroticism; the initials provide a neat **acronym** to act as a **mnemonic** – OCEAN
Blindsight	A condition caused by damage to the visual cortex, in which a person can be shown to respond to visual stimuli without consciously perceiving them
Body mass index (BMI)	A formula that assesses the weight of a person according to their height in order to provide an estimate of the extent to which they are over- or underweight; it is calculated by dividing the weight in kilograms by the square of the height in metres
Boolean search	A method of searching the web that enables you to make your search more precise by using the terms 'and', 'and not' and/or 'or' before your keywords
Case study	An empirical inquiry that investigates a phenomenon within its real-life context; in clinical work, it refers to a report of an individual patient or client
Classical conditioning	A kind of learning first described in dogs by Pavlov, which is simply dependent on the association of stimuli and responses in the right arrangement; much advertising, which uses the association of a neutral or even harmful product with an attractive but irrelevant context to make us want to buy that product, depends on the belief that humans can be conditioned too; see also **Operant conditioning**
Clever Hans effect	The tendency of participants, particularly animals, to use cues given to them, perhaps unconsciously, by the experimenter to achieve a misleading result; so called after a famous German horse called Hans, who had apparently been trained to perform complex arithmetical calculations, giving the answer by tapping his hoof; the psychologist Oskar Pfungst (1911) demonstrated after prolonged study that Hans was responding to the unconscious body language of his trainer, a maths teacher, which was telling him when to stop tapping

Cognitive behavioural therapy (CBT)	A psychological therapy that emphasizes the need to change the way a client is thinking about themselves and their situation
Cognitive dissonance theory	The idea, first proposed by Festinger (1957), that when some of our experiences, beliefs, attitudes feelings or actions are inconsistent with each other we find this unpleasant, and reinterpret or change them to make them consistent
Collusion	Occurs when two or more students consciously collaborate in producing work that is then submitted by each as their own effort, unless this has been formally condoned as a group project, in which case it is viewed as collaboration; this is likely to be picked up by plagiarism software such as **Turnitin**
Conditioning	See **Classical conditioning** and **Operant conditioning**
Confidence rating	A judgement, usually using a **Likert scale**, of how certain a participant is about a decision he has made; important, for example, in evaluating the accuracy of eye-witness testimony where it has been shown that the more confident a witness is the more likely their recall is to be accurate (Roberts & Higham, 2002)
Constancy	The property of our perceptual system that enables us to perceive things as unchanging when the stimulus generating that perception is changing – for example, by changing its distance from us
Content analysis	A systematic, replicable technique for compressing many words of text into fewer content categories based on explicit rules of coding
Déjà vu	The, incorrect, feeling that you have encountered or experienced an event before
Demand characteristics	The tendency of participants in experiments to produce the results they or the experimenter are expecting to achieve, or sometimes – just to annoy – the opposite of these
Depth of processing hypothesis	The idea that the deeper the level of processing during learning the better the subsequent retention and retrieval
Digital object identifier (DOI)	A number that provides an identification for a document on the web, which is more permanent than the web address and enables you to localize the document even if it has moved to a new website (see also Appendix 1)
Discourse analysis	A general term for a number of approaches to analysing written, spoken or signed language use

Displacement activity	Activity, often trivial like tidying your desk, which you do instead of the priority task, like writing that assignment (actually, a term from animal behaviour where animals do something apparently irrelevant in the face of two conflicting motivations – for example, preening behaviour in the chaffinch when in an approach-avoidance conflict)
Distal (see also *Proximal*)	Further from centre of body
Dose response curve	The relationship, expressed most clearly graphically, between the level of a treatment (the dose of a drug) and the size of the effect of that drug (the response); often used metaphorically for non-drug-related treatments
Double blind	An experimental design where neither the participant nor the researcher running the experiment knows what the condition is – for example, when comparing the performance of a group taking a drug with those taking a **placebo**; it avoids biasing the results because of **experimenter bias**, **observer bias** or **demand characteristics**
Dyslexia	A specific learning disability that manifests primarily as a difficulty with written language, particularly with reading and spelling
Empirical/ empirically	Based on observation or **experiment**; contrasting with 'philosophical', which implies not based on evidence but relying solely on logical argument
Ethical approval	There is a requirement to obtain formal approval for any research involving humans or their personal data; obtaining this will require evidence of adequate procedures for ensuring that participants have given their **informed consent** and that all risks have been considered and minimized (see pages 143–144)
European Computer Driving Licence (ECDL)	A qualification for general skills in ICT, which your university may offer free to all its students; it consists of seven modules – Concepts of Information Technology, Using the Computer and Managing Files, Word processing, Spreadsheets, Databases, Presentation, and Information and Communication; not difficult and looks good on your CV
Experiment	Research where data are collected to test a particular **hypothesis**
Experimenter bias	The tendency for experimenters to bias the results of an experiment towards the expected or desired outcome; this is a particular danger in **qualitative research**

Fabrication	The invention of data; the most infamous case in psychology being Cyril Burt's twin studies (Mackintosh, 1995)
Factor analysis	The statistical technique of identifying a small number of factors that can account for differences in behaviour – for example, variations in personality; fun is had in then naming these factors; it all looks like magic until you understand the underlying maths
False negative	Failing to report the presence of a stimulus; for example, missing your friend's face in a crowd
False positive	Incorrectly reporting the presence of a stimulus that is not present; for example, seeing a ghost
Flash bulb memories	Remarkably vivid and seemingly permanent memories typical of highly emotional and personal events in one's life; they can also be of personal circumstances during an event that did not affect one personally, such as a leader's assassination or 9/11
Folk (or naïve) psychology	Everyday usage of psychological ideas, concepts and terms, often based on no or little evidence; for example, 'redheads have short tempers'; racist and sexist assertions fall into this category
Forced choice	An experimental procedure where the participant has to choose one of two or more alternatives; they are not allowed to say they do not know (multiple-choice test exams work on the same principle); it is a way of getting at the underlying knowledge or ability independently of confidence levels
Free recall	Condition when no cues are given to assist information retrieval, and the participant organizes the information by memory, often revealing the mental processes used
Gender, gender role and gender identity	The behaviour (role) or feelings (identity) society and individuals associate with being male or female; to be distinguished from *sex*
General intelligence (g)	A term coined by Spearman to express the idea that there is a common factor in all kinds of mental ability tests; in addition to specific mental abilities, which he labelled 's'
Genes	The inherited instructions for our physical (and therefore behavioural) development, coded in the molecular structure of DNA; see also **Meme**
Gestalt	The idea that the whole is greater than the sum of the parts; it was applied particularly to the way in which we form meaningful visual perceptions of individual shapes from complex overlapping arrays of visual stimuli; a

group, working in the 1930s in Germany and then in the United States, developed a set of laws or principles to define how this occurred; Gestalt is the German word for form or shape, but since these do not capture the subtlety of the idea it is left untranslated, giving non-German speakers effectively a new word for a new idea

Graduate Basis for Registration (GBR)
Postgraduate training courses for applied areas of the discipline – clinical, educational, forensic, etc. – require you to have obtained GBR by graduating from an undergraduate degree accredited by the BPS with a 2:2 (lower-second) class degree or better

Grounded theory
A method developed by researchers in the 1960s, particularly Glaser and Strauss (1967), for doing **qualitative** data analysis involving the systematic generation of theory from data, and formulating hypotheses from conceptual ideas

Halo effect
The bias that we are prone to, of assuming that a person with one good characteristic is good on all other dimensions too; for example, the belief that attractive people are intelligent

Hawthorne effect
An experimental artefact in which participants respond to the investigator's attention rather than the specific variable being investigated; it was first observed at the Hawthorne plant of the Western Electric Company in Chicago in 1927–29, where any change the experimenter made in working conditions seemed to produce an increase in productivity; the term was probably first coined by Henry Landsberger (1958); it is particularly important in evaluating the effectiveness of an intervention or treatment in clinical, occupational and educational psychology

Heritability
The proportion of the variation in behavioural traits – for example intelligence – between individuals, that can be accounted for by genetic factors

Hypothesis
The prediction you make before you do research, based on previous studies, theory or just whim, and that your research is designed to test; see also **Experimental hypothesis** and **Null hypothesis** in Appendix 5

Informed consent
The procedure for ensuring that participants understand exactly what they will have to do in the research they are helping you with and that they have voluntarily given their consent to take part; this is a crucial requirement for obtaining **ethical approval** for research

Instrumental conditioning	See *Operant conditioning*
Intelligence quotient (IQ)	A measure of intelligence adjusted for the average performance of others in the age group being tested; this average is assigned the score of 100 with a standard deviation of 15; originally defined as mental/physical age × 100
Internet	A worldwide, publicly accessible series of interconnected computer networks that carries the **World Wide Web**
Intranet	An internet computer network that is private to an organization and controlled by internal protocols
Introspection	The self-observation and reporting of conscious inner thoughts, desires and sensations
Inverted U-shaped curve	A graphical metaphor for something that increases up to a certain point and then falls off – for example, hunger when presented with an unlimited supply of chocolate bars and forced to eat them; see also **Yerkes–Dodson Law**
Journal	Where most new ideas, theories and research results are first published; these are soft-bound publications, like magazines but without the pretty pictures, that appear at regular intervals; a certain number of these issues will make up a volume, which will be collected and bound up into a hard cover to put on your library's shelves; every **paper** in a journal will have a specific **reference**; most journals now appear in electronic form as well as in hard copy, so can be found on the web if your library subscribes to them; a few new journals are now published only electronically
Levels of explanation	The idea that the same phenomenon can be investigated, described and explained at different levels using different kinds of language; so memory can be explained in terms of neural mechanisms or cognitive processes or computational models; one is not better than the other – they are just different; the long-term goal is to bring them together into a unified theory
Likert scale	Originally a response scale used in questionnaires, where the participant indicates whether they agree or disagree with a statement by ringing a number on a scale:

STRONGLY DISAGREE   1—2—3—4—5   STRONGLY AGREE

Now commonly used to describe similar scales for rating other dimensions – for example:

ATTRACTIVE   1—2—3—4—5   UNATTRACTIVE

One important use is in determining **confidence ratings**; the number of points on the scale can vary – five, seven and nine are the most commonly used; if it is desirable to avoid the respondent sitting on the fence, neither agreeing nor disagreeing, then an even-numbered scale is used; this is a form of **forced choice**; see also **Visual analogue scale**

Long-term memory	The stage of memory in which large amounts of information are stored for extended periods; see *Short-term memory*
Meme	A term coined by Richard Dawkins (1976) to describe a unit of cultural information like a habit, tune, design or idea, which gets transmitted through society, evolving as it spreads through a process analogous to **natural selection**; it is the cultural equivalent of a **gene**
Mere exposure	A phenomenon, first described by Robert Zajonc in the 1960s (see Zajonc, 2001), in which the simple repetition of a stimulus, like someone's face or a piece of music, results in increased liking of that stimulus; this is one of the keystone assumptions underlying much advertising
Metacognition	The ability of an individual to reflect on his or her own thinking and consequently to improve their intellectual performance
Mnemonic	A strategy for learning information by placing it in an arbitrary but systematic context like a familiar location
Modularity	'The modularity of mind' was a phrase (and a book title) coined by Jerry Fodor (1983) to express the idea that different mental functions (spatial memory, verbal memory, colour vision, spatial vision, etc.) are processed by different and independent structures
Natural selection	The term coined by Charles Darwin (1859) to describe the process underlying evolution in which the features of an organism that help it survive and reproduce are more likely to be passed on to subsequent generations and therefore become more common
Observer	A more neutral description of the **participants** in an experiment when they are being asked to make some kind of visual discrimination
Observer bias	The tendency of observers to bias their observations towards the expected or desired effect
Occam's/Ockham's razor	A principle named after the fourteenth-century English monk William of Ockham, which says that we should

	always prefer the simplest explanation of a phenomenon; this is particularly important in explanations of human motivation where, perhaps to preserve our dignity, we often attribute elaborate, high-flown motives to, for example, simple greed
Operant conditioning	A kind of learning where an action is followed by a reward and this causes the action to be repeated; examples are pigeons learning to press a lever if this results in a food pellet, or children learning to sit still if they are praised for this; also known as instrumental conditioning; see also **Classical conditioning**
Paper	As well as the product made from cutting down trees, this refers to an article in a **journal**; every paper is identified by a specific **reference**; most papers now appear in electronic form as well as, or even instead of, in hard copies, which saves on trees
Paradigm	A conceptual framework within which theories are constructed
Parapsychology	The scientific study of paranormal phenomena
Participants	The euphemism for describing the poor sods you have dragooned into taking part in your experiment; we used to call them **subjects** – they still often do in the USA; is that significant?
Peer review	This is the 'kite mark' of quality in **journal** articles and the reason why they are a much more reliable source of evidence (though of course still not perfect) than random material harvested from the web; all good journals will send articles submitted to them out to at least two reputable researchers in the field who will advise the editor of the journal whether or not the article should be published; even if they generally approve of an article, they will often recommend that more or different analyses of the data, or even more experiments, are done before final acceptance; this may lead to a dialogue between the authors and the reviewers until agreement is achieved
Phenomenology	The study of consciousness as experienced from the first-person point of view; a process dependent on **introspection**
Placebo effect	The alteration in behaviour or symptoms produced by a pharmacologically inert drug; this can be generalized to the psychological or medical effects of any treatment,

	which occur simply because the patient or client believes the treatment will have an effect; it is therefore important to control for this general effect in evaluating any outcomes; see also **Hawthorne effect**
Portal (or web portal)	A site that functions as a point of access to information on the **World Wide Web**; your university may have a specially designed student portal that gives you access to those parts of its **intranet** that will be useful to you; you might consider making it your home page – at least during term time
Proximal	Nearer to the centre of the body
PsychINFO	An electronic bibliographic database of the American Psychological Association (APA), which provides abstracts and citations for the research literature in the behavioural sciences and mental health
Psychoanalysis	A method for investigating mental processes, which assumes the existence of a psychic unconscious and uses analysis as a therapeutic procedure
Psychopharmacology	The study of drug-induced changes in mood, sensation, thinking and behaviour
Qualitative research	The investigation of a phenomenon using the analysis of descriptive accounts to identify patterns in human behaviour
Quantitative research	The investigation of a phenomenon using measurement or at least relative judgements of the strength of that phenomenon
q.v. ('quod vide')	Literally 'which see' – used to direct the reader to another part of the publication
Rapid eye movements	Phases of sleep that are characterized by REM sleep are physiologically distinct and associated with most recalled dreams
Receptive field	The receptor area that, when stimulated, results in a response of a particular sensory neuron; each sensory neuron has its own unique receptive field
Recognition memory	The ability to remember whether or not a stimulus or event has been encountered before; **déjà vu** is a false recognition memory
Reference	This is how you find, or identify in your own essays, a particular book or **paper** in a **journal**; so the reference: Bertamini, M., Latto, R. & Spooner, A. (2003) The Venus effect: people's understanding of mirror reflections in paintings. *Perception, 32*(5), 593–599.

	identifies a paper published in pages 593–599 of issue number 5 in volume 32 of the journal *Perception*, which was published in the year 2003 (see also Appendix 1 on how to structure a reference)
Reliability	The extent to which a test or measure is consistent in producing the same result on repeated use in the same situation, to be distinguished from **validity**
Retrograde amnesia	**Amnesia** for events prior to the trauma – a head injury, for example – that caused the amnesia; see also **Anterograde amnesia**
Sex	The term used to refer to whether a person or animal has male or female biological and physical characteristics; to be distinguished from **gender, gender role and gender identity**
Short-term memory	A stage of memory in which a small amount of information is stored for only a short time – seconds rather than minutes – unless it is rehearsed; also known as **Working memory**; see also **Long-term memory**
Signal detection theory (SDT)	The theory that when we perceive something (like a friend's face in a crowd) it is the result of a decision about whether a particular stimulus (a face) belongs to a signal (the friend) or the background noise (the crowd); this decision is affected by two things – our sensitivity (in the example, our eyesight) and our bias (whether we are expecting to see our friend or not); sensitivity is usually represented by the symbol d′ (pronounced d prime) and bias by the Greek letter β (pronounced beta)
Simulation	Imitation of a real situation, object or process – for example, using actors to simulate a crime
State-dependent memory	Memory enhanced by particular conditions or cues, usually the one in which the event being recalled occurred
Statistical Package for the Social Sciences (SPSS)	Usually known to its friends as SPSS; the software that enables us to analyse our data and display it graphically
Subjects	The old term used to describe the people taking part in your experiment, often abbreviated to Ss; use **participants** or **observers** instead
SWOT analysis	A useful framework for analysing a situation, or even yourself, by identifying Strengths, Weaknesses, Opportunities and Threats
Tertium quid	Literally 'a third thing', which might be responsible for an apparent correlation between two other factors (e.g.

the apparent link between weight and seniority might be due to the fact that they are both associated with age – see Experiment 1, page 156); note that Latin words and expressions like this can be put in italics – which also makes them jump out of the page to impress your tutor!

Theory of mind (ToM)	The ability, found at least in humans and the other apes, to accurately attribute mental states, such as particular beliefs, knowledge or desires, to others: 'I know you know . . .'
Thought experiment	The use of a hypothetical scenario to help us understand the way things actually are; they are more popular with philosophers than psychologists, who like to get their hands dirty actually collecting evidence
Trait theory	The attempt to account for variations in aspects of behaviour, particularly personality, in terms of a limited number of factors – for example, the **Big Five**, which are identified by **factor analysis**; these traits are assumed to be relatively permanent once established but may initially be the result of either inherited characteristics or environmental factors
Turnitin	Online plagiarism and collusion detection software
Typo	Something to avoid; the jargon your tutor may use for careless typing and formatting mistakes in your course-work that will lose you marks, however brilliant the intellectual content; short for 'typographical errors'
Uniform resource locator (URL)	The location of a document on the **World Wide Web**, i.e. a web address – always referred to as a URL
Validity	The extent to which a test or observation measures what it is supposed to measure; to be distinguished from **reliability**
Visual analogue scale (VAS)	Like a **Likert scale**, these are used for rating the strength of a dimension; instead of having numbers to indicate strength, the participant is simply presented with a line to mark:

ATTRACTIVE _____ UNATTRACTIVE

The experimenter then measures the position of the participant's mark on the line; this generates continuous data (see Appendix 5), which allow more powerful statistical tests to be used

Web of Knowledge (WoK)	A web-based database where users can search across almost all academic **journals** and many books

Working memory   See **Short-term memory**

World Wide Web   System of interlinked hypertext documents accessed via the internet, created in 1989 by Sir Tim Berners-Lee

Yerkes–Dodson Law   The empirical observation that, in many situations, increasing arousal levels produce increased performance up to a certain point, after which performance deteriorates (Yerkes & Dodson, 1908); so, for any particular task, there is an optimum level of performance (see Figure 2.3 and **Inverted U-shaped curve**)

Appendix 5 Common terms (and some of their alternatives) used in statistics

Standard abbreviations are shown in brackets. Note these are usually in italics, which is tedious for typing, but that is the convention. (They do also vary between textbooks, so check in the list of symbols you find in the book you are using.) *Words in italics have their own definition.*

Examples of how to report the results of some of the common statistical tests are given, under the test entry, in square brackets.

For more terms used in experimental design and methodology, see Appendix 4.

Alpha (α) level	The level of *probability* at which you decide in advance the *null hypothesis* can be rejected and you can announce that you have a significant result; it is usually set at 0.001, 0.001 or 0.05; in behavioural experiments, where we typically have a large *variance*, we tend to choose 0.05, the easiest of these to achieve [$p < .05$]
Analysis of variance (ANOVA)	Probably the most common test used in psychology; use it when you have several *variables* or more than two groups and you want to compare their means. [The duration of eye contacts between individuals varied over the three conditions, $F(2, 177) = 4.37$, $p = .03$. (In this example the numbers 2 and 177 represent the *degrees of freedom*.).] Note the ANOVA does not tell you which conditions produced longer or shorter durations, just that there was a difference. You can get some idea of the direction of the difference by looking at the means, but to confirm that these are significant you would have to use planned *contrasts* or comparisons (if these were identified in advance) or *post hoc tests* (if the comparisons were not planned in advance); these compare each pair of means separately; ANOVAs will also tell you whether *interactions* between *variables* are significant, which is often the most interesting and important part of the analysis

Average	Not a term used much in respectable statistical circles because there are different kinds of averages (*means*, *medians* and *modes*) for use in different situations, and we do not want to get them confused, do we?
Bar chart	A graphical way of representing *means*; see page 150
Bell-shaped curve	See *Normal distribution*
Between-group design	When each condition or treatment is used with a different group of participants; also known as an *independent design*
Bias	See Appendix 4
Box-and-whisker plot	See *Boxplot*
Boxplot	A graphical way of representing both the *median* and important aspects of the spread of the data around the median; see page 148 also known as a *box-and-whisker plot*
Categorical	If you are measuring something by putting it into two categories or more than two categories that are not necessarily the same size (for example, classifying people as Indian, Chinese, African or European), then the data you are collecting are categorical; categorial, which is the better word for this according to its dictionary definition, is only rarely used (psychologists may be both literate and numerate, but that is too much to expect of most statisticians); also known as nominal or frequency data; see also *Ordinal*, *Continuous* and *Contingency table*
Chi-square test (χ^2)	Pronounced ki, to rhyme with eye, and written with the Greek letter chi as χ^2; a useful test for analysing data where you have the frequencies of things falling into different categories. [$\chi^2(4, N = 90) = 10.51$, $p = .03$ (in this example, N is the total number of participants).]
Confidence interval	If you calculate the *mean* of a *sample*, then the 95% confidence interval is the range or spread of values around that mean which would, with a 95% probability, contain the mean of the *population* from which that population was drawn (i.e. the true value of the mean you are trying to discover); so it is telling you how confident you can be in the mean you have obtained from your observations; nothing in science is ever certain, but some things are more probable than others
Confidence rating	See Appendix 4
Confounding variable	This is something we are all desperately trying to avoid in our own results and desperately trying to find in other people's – especially if they contradict our theories; it

describes something, other than the *independent variable* you are investigating, that is affecting the *dependent variable* you are measuring; it is sometimes just called a confound; they are often the result of bad experimental design – for example, if you are comparing the effects of solving a problem alone and in a social group and you test all the participants on task A working alone and then on task B working in groups; there are two confounds which will prevent you drawing any sensible conclusions – (a) task difficulty (task A may be easier or more difficult than task B) and (b) an order effect (boredom or fatigue may make people worse on task B or practice might make them better); these could have been avoided by *counterbalancing*

Contingency table   If you have two or more *categorical* variables they can be arranged in a contingency table to help analyse the distribution across the different categories; suppose we are looking at the effect of a regular intake of a new cognitive enhancer 'iQ' on student performance, we could have one categorical variable of iQ taking (two categories, yes or no) and another of degree class (five categories) and produce a table of the numbers of students in each category, as follows:

Drug taken	Degree class obtained					Total
	1	2.1	2.2	3	Fail	
iQ	25	123	54	23	3	228
Placebo	35	145	43	19	2	244
Total	60	268	97	42	5	472

We could then test for the significance of the effect, perhaps using a *chi-square test*

Continuous   A kind of *variable*, like age or height, that can in theory take any value between the smallest and the largest points on the scale; also called Interval to describe the situation (more common than absolutely continuous data) when you put things into different categories that are of the same size and in a specific order – for example, year of birth; these are effectively interchangeable terms and the data are treated the same in statistics; see also *Categorical* and *Ordinal*

Contrasts	A set of comparisons between group means performed after an *ANOVA* has identified a significant effect; they are used when you have planned these comparisons in advance to test a particular theory or hypothesis; they are more powerful (see *Power*) than *post hoc tests*
Correlation	The extent to which two measurements vary together; for example, as children get older their height increases, so height is correlated with age; this is a positive correlation; in old age, on the other hand, height gradually decreases; this is a negative correlation
Correlation coefficient	The measurement of the strength of the correlation. It can vary from 0 (no correlation) to 1 (perfect correlation); there are a number of different ways of calculating a correlation between two variables; see, for example, *Pearson's correlation coefficient*
Counterbalancing	A way of designing your experiment or observation to avoid the effects of *confounding variables*; so, in the example given in that entry, the *participants* should have been divided into four groups to be tested in four different ways (A group, B alone; B alone, A group; A alone, B group; B group, A alone); then when all the data are put together the effects of the possible confounding variables will be balanced out
Data	These are what we are all desperately seeking. It can be either *qualitative* or *quantitative* but it is always plural; never say 'The data is . . .'
Degrees of freedom (*df*)	Even Andy Field (2005) says this is impossible to define in less than a few pages, but it is a number you need to know when working out the probability level of the value of a particular statistic (*F* or *t*, etc.); they are derived from the number of participants in your groups, but, do not worry, SPSS will calculate them for you, as well as telling you what the probability level is
Dependent variable	The dimension or property you are measuring in your experiment; sometimes called the *outcome variable*; if you were measuring the effect of different volumes of music on learning neuroanatomy, volume would be the independent variable; number of anatomical terms learnt would be the dependent variable
Descriptive statistics	The presentation of your results in tables and graphs; they do not include statements about differences, correlations, etc. – these are part of the *inferential statistics*

Effect size	An effect may be significant but tiny, particularly if the sample size is very large, or it may be significant and very large; the actual size of an effect can be measured in a number of ways, including Cohen's *d*, Glass's *g* and *Pearson's correlation coefficient (r)*
Error bars	A way of representing the variation in your data (see page 151); the length of an error bar can represent either the 95% *confidence interval*, the *standard error* or, more rarely, the *standard deviation*; it is important that you say which in the legend of your figure
Experimental hypothesis (H₁)	The prediction that an experiment is testing
Factor	See *Independent variable*
Factor analysis	See Appendix 4
Forced choice	See Appendix 4
General linear model (GLM)	A term beyond the scope of this book (and us), which statisticians use to describe the procedures underlying some statistical tests; most importantly, SPSS uses the term GLM in its drop-down menus, giving you access to more complicated analyses of variance such as *MANOVAs*
Goodness-of-fit	As the name suggests, this is a measure of how well a theoretical model (for example, that the amount eaten is directly proportional to the length of time since the last meal) fits the data you have collected
Histogram	A way of plotting the frequencies with which different values of a dependent variable occur (see page 149); also known as a frequency distribution
Independent design	See *Between-group design*
Independent variable	The dimension or property you are manipulating in order to measure its effect; sometimes called a *Predictor variable* or a *Factor*; see also *Dependent variable*
Inferential statistics	Drawing conclusions from our *descriptive statistics* about differences, correlations, etc., which are supported by the results of statistical tests
Insignificant	Never, ever use this word when reporting statistical results. The correct term is non-significant (*ns*) or, better still, you can just say something is 'not significant'
Interaction	The way in which two or more different variables combine (i.e. interact) to affect the *variables* you are measuring (see Figure 5.4 for an example)
Interval	See *Continuous*
Mean (*M* or *x̄*)	The kind of average we are most familiar with; it is

	calculated by adding together all the scores and dividing by the number of scores; thus, the mean of 1,2,2,3,3,3, 3,4,4,5,7,11,58,63,92 is 17.4
Median (*Mdn*)	Another kind of average; it refers to the middle score of a set of ordered scores; thus, the median of 1,2,2,3,3,3,3, 4,4,5,7,11,58,63,92 is 4; when there is no unique middle value, it takes the midpoint between the two middle values
Mode	The most frequently occurring score; thus, the mode of 1,2,2,3,3,3,3,4,4,5,7,11,58,63,92 is 3
Multivariate analysis of variance (MANOVA)	An extension of the basic *ANOVA* to deal with situations where there is more than one *dependent variable*
Non-parametric test	The class of statistical tests you can use when data are *categorical* or *ordinal*, or when they are *continuous* but do not fit a normal distribution; they have less *power* than *parametric* tests, so are less likely to give you a significant result
Normal distribution	When the measurement being made varies in a symmetrical way around a mean value producing a classic *bell-shaped curve*; it is found when measuring almost any aspect of human behaviour (see the example in the diagram below)

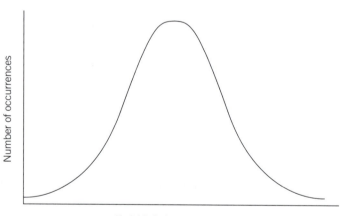

Variable being measured

If it is not symmetrical because it has a longer tail in one direction than the other, then it is said to be *skewed*

Null hypothesis (H$_0$)   The opposite of the *experimental hypothesis*; so it is the

	suggestion that the prediction made by the experimental hypothesis is wrong; statistical tests calculate the *probability* that the null hypothesis is correct
One-tailed test	The kind of test you use when your *experimental hypothesis* predicts, for a good evidence or theory based reason, the direction of an effect – for example, if you predict that girls will be better than boys on a vocabulary test because you have other evidence that they do better on related linguistic tests; to convert a two-tailed probability given by a statistical test to a one-tailed one, you simply halve it; so you are more likely to get a significant result with a one-tailed test; see also *Two-tailed test*
Opportunity sample	When you go into the coffee bar to persuade people to take part in your experiment this is an opportunity sample of participants, not a *random* sample
Ordinal	The kind of data you get when you put things into categories that may be of different size but have a meaningful order; classifying degrees as firsts, upper seconds, etc. is an example of this; see also *Categorical* and *Continuous*
Outcome variable	See *Dependent variable*
Outlier	An observation or measurement that you might consider excluding from your analysis because it is clearly very different from the rest of the data; in experiments that measure reaction times, for example, there will probably be a few trials on which the *participant* blinks or even nods off, giving an abnormally long reaction time, which can with good justification be excluded; *boxplots* are a good way of looking at the pattern of data to see if there are outliers distorting the data (see example in Figure 5.1)
Parametric test	The class of test you use when the data are continuous and follow a *normal distribution*; examples are *analysis of variance* and *t-tests*; see also *Non-parametric test*
Pearson's correlation coefficient (*r*)	Or Pearson's product-moment correlation; the most commonly used measure of the relationship (*correlation*) between two variables. [Exam performance was negatively related to the amount drunk the night before ($r = -.63$, $p < .001$).] It is also a useful measure of *effect size*
Population	The whole group of people that you are investigating by collecting data from a *sample* of them
Post hoc tests	Comparisons of pairs of means in a design where there are more than two means and an *analysis of variance* has shown there are overall differences between the means;

commonly used post hoc tests are the *t-test*, Bonferroni's test and Tukey's test; post hoc is Latin for 'after this', and these tests are typically used when you have not made a prediction about group differences in advance; if you have predicted particular differences, then you can use the trickier, but more powerful (see *Power*) planned *contrasts* (in practice people often use post hoc tests for making planned comparisons because although they are slightly less likely to give you a significant result, they are thought to be easier to use)

Power	A measure of the ability of a test to detect an effect of a particular size (see *Effect size*)
Predictor variable	See *Independent variable*
Probability (*p*)	The chance of something occurring; it can be expressed on a scale from 0 (never) to 1 (always), or 0% to 100%; so a probability of 0.5 is the same as a probability of 50%
Qualitative	When the data you are collecting are descriptive, at least to begin with; if you classify or categorize qualitative data, they become *categorical*; qualitative data are often concerned with discovering 'meaning' rather than testing the truth of preset hypotheses
Quantitative	When the data you are collecting are numerical, either *categorical*, *ordinal* or *continuous*, right from the beginning
Random	This has a very specific meaning and refers to situations that are systematically randomized, perhaps by using random numbers generated by a computer; so when you go into the coffee bar to persuade people to take part in your experiment you are creating a far from random *sample*; see *Opportunity sample*
Raw scores (aka raw data)	These are the actual numbers you collect from your participants and feed into SPSS; you would not normally report them in your results section, where a summary in the form of means and standard deviations should be used (the one exception is *scatterplots*, which do show raw data); in a project report they might be included as an appendix
Reliability	The extent to which a test or measurement produces consistent results when used repeatedly
Sample (*N* or *n*)	When you make observations or run an experiment you want to find out about the whole *population* of that kind of person or animal; in practice, what you have to do is observe or test just a small (hopefully representative)

sample of that population; the selection of this sample can be crucial – for example, if you were taking an opinion poll and questioned only people in London, this would tell you something about the views of people in Knightsbridge but little about the views of the country as a whole; sometimes, though, it is not very crucial – when you read journal articles in many areas of psychology, of which cognitive is a good example, you will find that the *participants* are often undergraduate students and it is assumed, not unreasonably, that for the particular variables being measured these are representative of the population as a whole; in reporting sample sizes you can use the abbreviation N for the total number of participants tested and the abbreviation n for the number in each subgroup

Scatterplot	A useful way of plotting *raw data* to look for *correlations* between two variables (see Figure 5.5 page 152)
Skewed	See *Normal distribution*
Standard deviation (*SD* or σ)	An estimate of the spread of a set of data; it is the square root of the *variance*
Standard error (*SE* or σ_x)	The *standard deviation* of the *samples* taken from a particular *population*; sometimes referred to as the standard error of the mean (SEM); see *Variance*
Standardization	The process of converting a set of data into a standard form – for example, with a *mean* of zero and a *standard deviation* of ten; it allows you to compare two sets of data that use different measurement techniques; you may also come across it in the way your department treats examination marks, particularly from multiple-choice tests – because these can vary in difficulty, with one set of questions failing everybody and another giving everyone a first, the raw marks are often standardized to give a more acceptable distribution of marks; see also *z-score*
Sum (Σ)	The sum of a set of numbers, represented by the Greek letter sigma
t-test	A commonly used *parametric* test for comparing two *means*; the value calculated is sometimes referred to as Student's *t*; it is called this not because it is more friendly to students than many tests, though it is, but because it was invented by an employee of the Guinness brewery in Dublin, who published it under the pseudonym 'Student'. [The girls in my sample were taller than the boys, $t(75) =$

	2.11, $p = .04$. (two-tailed). (In this example, the *degrees of freedom* are 75.).]
Two-tailed test	The kind of statistical test you use when you are not predicting the direction of an effect or difference – for example, if you were asking whether there is a difference in the performance of boys and girls on a vocabulary test; see also *One-tailed test*
Validity	The extent to which a test or measurement assesses what it claims to measure
Variable	See *Dependent variable* and *Independent variable*
Variance (s^2 or σ^2)	An estimate of the variability or spread in a set of data; other related but different terms you will come across are *standard deviation* and *standard error*; see your statistics textbook for how to calculate all these; in general terms, the lower the variance the more reliable your data
z-score	A way of expressing the value of an observation in terms of the *standard deviation* of the set of data from which it has come; doing this for the whole set produces a new distribution with a mean of zero and a standard deviation of one; this is a form of *standardization*

Appendix 6

Further reading

Here are some additional sources that we think you might find useful if you want to know more about some particular aspect of study. Your psychology department may also make specific recommendations in some of these areas.

General

Frith C.D. (2007). *Making up the mind: How the brain creates our mental world.* Oxford, U.K.: Blackwell Publishing.
A very readable short introduction to many of the topics you will cover during your psychology degree.

Schachter, D.L., Gilbert, T.L., & Wegner, D.M. (2009). *Psychology.* New York, U.S.A.: Worth Publishers.
Opinions vary on this, but a large general introduction can be a useful starting point in understanding a topic. If your department recommends one, buy it. If not, this new book from three distinguished Harvard professors is both entertaining and authoritative.

University

Sinclair, C. (2006). *Understanding university: A guide to another planet.* Berkshire, U.K.: Open University Press.

Writing

Levin, P. (2004). *Write great essays!* Berkshire, U.K.: Open University Press.
Smyth, T.R. (2004). *The principles of writing in psychology.* Basingstoke, U.K.: Palgrave MacMillan.

Research practicals and projects

Berg, B. (2006). *Qualitative research methods for the social sciences* (6th ed.). Boston, U.S.A.: Pearson/Alleyn & Bacon
Forshaw, M. (2005). *Doing research projects in psychology: A practical guide.* Oxford, U.K.: Blackwell Publishing.
Reason, P., & Bradbury, H. (Eds.). 2008. *The SAGE handbook of action research: Participative inquiry and practice.* London, U.K.: Sage.
Shaughnessy, J.J., Zechmeister, E.B., & Zechmeister, J.S. (2006). *Research methods in psychology* (7th ed.). New York, U.S.A.: McGraw-Hill.

Statistics

Field, A. (2005). *Discovering statistics using SPSS,* (2nd ed.) London, U.K.: Sage Publications

Referencing

Publication Manual of the American Psychological Association (5th ed.). (2001). Washington DC, U.S.A.: American Psychological Association
Purdue University Online Writing Lab (OWL) (March 27, 2008) *Using American Psychological Association (APA) format.* Retrieved April 8, 2008, from http://owl.english.purdue.edu/handouts/research/r_apa.html

Planning ahead

Lanz, C., Moysey, L., Dean, L., Tause, L., & Duncan, A. (2008). *Psychology student employability guide*. York, U.K.: The Higher Education Academy Psychology Network.

Psychology of Education

Blakemore, S.J., & Frith, U. (2005). *The learning brain: Lessons for education*. Oxford, U.K.: Blackwell Publishing.

Dictionaries and Encyclopaedias

Useful for concise and authoritative introductions to topics
Colman, A. (Ed.). (2006). *Oxford dictionary of psychology*. Oxford, U.K.: Oxford University Press.
Davey, G. (Ed.). (2006). *Encyclopaedic dictionary of psychology*. London, U.K.: Hodder Arnold.
Gregory, R.L. (Ed.). (2004). *The Oxford companion to the mind* (2nd ed.). Oxford, U.K.: Oxford University Press.
Roeckelein, J.E. (Ed.). (2006). *Elsevier's dictionary of psychological theories* . Amsterdam, The Netherlands: Elsevier.
VandenBos, G.R. (Ed.). (2006). *APA dictionary of psychology*. Washington D.C., U.S.A.: American Psychological Association.

References

Aserinsky, E., & Kleitman, N. (1953). Regularly occurring periods of eye motility, and concomitant phenomena, during sleep. *Science, 118*, 273–274.

Bales, R.F (1958). Task roles and social roles in problem solving groups. In Maccoby, E. (Ed.), *Readings in social psychology* (3rd ed., pp. 437–447). New York, U.S.A.: Holt, Rhinehart & Winston.

Banister, P., Burman, E., Parker, I., Taylor, M., & Tindall, C. (1997). *Qualitative methods in psychology: a research guide*. Buckingham, U.K.: Open University Press.

Bensley, D.A (2008). Can you learn to think more like a psychologist? *The Psychologist, 21*, 128–129.

Berg, B. (2006). *Qualitative research methods for the social sciences* (6th ed.). Boston, U.S.A.: Pearson/Alleyn & Bacon.

Blakemore, S.J., & Frith, U. (2005). *The learning brain*. Oxford, U.K.: Blackwell.

Born, J., Rasch, B., & Gais, S. (2006). Sleep to remember. *Neuroscientist, 12*(5), 410–424.

Bramwell, R., West, H., & Salmon, P. (2006). Health professionals' and service users' interpretation of screening test results: experimental study. *British Medical Journal, 333*, 284–288.

Broadbent, D. (1961). *Behaviour*. London, U.K: Methuen.

Butler, A.C., & Roediger, H.L. (2007). Testing improves long-term retention in a simulated classroom setting. *European Journal of Cognitive Psychology, 19*, 514–527.

Carroll, L. (1865). *Alice's adventures in wonderland*. London, U.K.: Macmillan.

Charmaz, K. (1995). Grounded theory. In J.A. Smith, R. Harré & L. Van Langenhove (Eds.), *Rethinking methods in psychology* (pp. 27–49). London, U.K.: Sage.

Darwin, C. (1859). *On the origin of species by means of natural selection*. London, U.K.: J. Murray.

Dawkins, R. (1976). *The selfish gene*. Oxford, U.K.: Oxford University Press.

Dunning, D., Heath, C., & Suls, J.M. (2004). Flawed self-assessment: Implications for health, education and business. *Psychological Science in the Public Interest, 5*(3), 69–106.

Festinger, L. (1957). *A theory of cognitive dissonance*. Stanford, California, U.S.A.: Stanford University Press.

Field, A. (2005). *Discovering statistics using SPSS* (2nd ed.). London, U.K.: Sage Publications.

Flavell, J.H. (1979). Metacognition and cognitive monitoring: A new area of cognitive-developmental inquiry. *The American Psychologist, 34*, 906–911.

Fodor, J. (1983). *Modularity of mind: An essay on faculty psychology*. Cambridge, U.S.A.: MIT Press.

Forster, E.M. (1976). *Aspects of the novel*. London: Penguin. (Originally published 1927)

Freud, S. (1991). *The interpretation of dreams* (New edited edn.). London: Penguin Books. (Originally published as *Die Traumdeutung*, 1899)

Fromm, E. (1979). *To have or to be?* (2nd ed.). London, U.K.: Sphere.

Gilovich, T., Medvec, V. H., & Savitsky, K. (2000). The spotlight effect in social judgment: An egocentric bias in estimates of the salience of one's own actions and appearance. *Journal of Personality and Social Psychology, 79*, 211–222.

Glaser, B. G., & Strauss, A. L. (1967). *The discovery of grounded theory: Strategies for Qualitative Research.* Chicago, Illinois, U.S.A.: Aldine Publishing Company.

Godden, D.R., & Baddeley, A.D. (1975). Context-dependent memory in two natural environments: On land and under water. *British Journal of Psychology, 66*, 325–331.

Goldberg, L. R. (1983). The structure of phenotypic personality trait. *American Psychologist, 48*, 26–34.

Grant, A.M., & Palmer, S. (2002). *Coaching Psychology.* Workshop and meeting held at the Annual Conference of the Division of Counselling Psychology, British Psychological Society, Torquay, 18 May.

Gregory, R.L. (1998). *Eye and brain* (5th edn.). Oxford: Oxford University Press.

Harris, J.E., & Morris, P.E. (Eds.). (1984). *Everyday memories, actions, and absentmindedness.* New York, U.S.A.: Academic Press.

Her Majesty's Stationery Office. (1997). *National committee of inquiry into higher education (The Dearing report)* (HMSO NCIHE 97/850). London, UK: HMSO.

Horswill, M. S., Waylen, A. E., & Tofield, M. I. (2004). Drivers' ratings of different components of their own driving skill: A greater illusion of superiority for skills that relate to accident involvement. *Journal of Applied Social Psychology, 34*(1), 177–195.

Israel, M., & Hay, I. (2006*). Research ethics for social scientists: Between ethical conduct and regulatory compliance.* London, U.K.: Sage.

Josephs,A.P., & Smithers, A.G. (1975). Personality characteristics of syllabus bound and syllabus free sixth formers. *British Journal of Educational Psychology, 45*(1), 29–38.

Kahneman, D., & Tversky, A. (1973). On the psychology of prediction. *Psychological Review, 80*, 237–25l.

Kolb, D.A. (1984). *Experiential learning: experience as the source of learning and development.* Englewood Cliffs, NJ, U.S.A.: Prentice Hall.

Landsberger, H. A. (1958). *Hawthorne Revisited.* Ithaca, NY, U.S.A.: Cornell University Press.

Layard, R. (2006).*The depression report.* London, U.K.: Mental Health Policy Group of the Centre for Economic Performance, London School of Economics.

Lea, S. (1999). *Psychological writing.* Exeter University, School of Psychology Web Site. Retrieved December 17, 2007 from http://www.people.ex.ac.uk/SEGLea/psy6002/writing.htm

Mackintosh N.J. (Ed.). (1995). *Cyril Burt: Fraud or framed?* Oxford, U.K.: Oxford University Press.

Maguire, E.A., Valentine, E.R., Wilding, J.M., & Kapur, N. (2003). Routes to remembering: The brains behind superior memory. *Nature Neuroscience, 6*, 90–95.

Maquet, P., Laureys S., Peigneux P., Fuchs S, Petiau C., Phillips C., et al. (2000). Experience-dependent changes in cerebral activation during human REM sleep. *Nature Neuroscience, 3*(8), 831–6.

McCartney, P. (2007). *Memory almost full* (Audio CD B000P2A242). London, U.K.: Mercury Records.

McDaniel, M.A., Anderson, J.L., Derbish, M.H., & Morrisette, N. (2007). Testing the testing effect in the classroom. *European Journal of Cognitive Psychology, 19*, 494–513.

Merriman, H.S. (1901). *The velvet glove* (chap. 16). Retrieved 20 December 2007 from http://www.gutenberg.org/files/10342/10342-h/10342-h.htm

Milgram, S. (1963). Behavioral study of obedience. *Journal of Abnormal and Social Psychology, 67,* 371–378.

Miller, H. (1957). *Big Sur and the oranges of Hieronymous Bosch.* New York, U.S.A.: New Directions Publishing Corporation.

Moore, D.A. (2007). Not so above average after all: When people believe they are worse than average and its implications for theories of bias in social comparison. *Organizational Behaviour and Human Decision Processes. 102,* 42–58.

Nijstad, B.A., Stroebe, W., & Lodewijkx, H.F.M. (2006). The illusion of group productivity: A reduction of failures explanation. *European Journal of Social Psychology, 36,* 31–48.

Pask, G (1988). Learning strategies, teaching strategies and conceptual learning style. In R.R. Schmeck (Ed.), *Learning strategies and learning style* (pp. 83–89). NewYork, U.S.A.: Plenum Press.

Pfungst, O. (1911). *Clever Hans (The horse of Mr. von Osten): A contribution to experimental animal and human psychology* (C. L. Rahn, Trans.). New York: Henry Holt. (Original work published in German 1907)

Pope, A. (2004). *An essay on criticism.* Whitefish, Montana, U.S.A.: Kessinger Publishing Co. (Originally published 1711)

Policy statement on a progress file for higher education. (2000). Gloucester, U.K.: Quality Assurance Agency for Higher Education.

Publication manual of the American Psychological Association (5th ed.). (2001). Washington, DC, U.S.A.: American Psychological Association.

Roberts, W.T., & Higham, P.A. (2002). Selecting accurate statements from the cognitive interview using confidence ratings. *Journal of Experimental Psychology: Applied, 8,* 33–43.

Smith, J. A. (1995). *Semi-structured interviewing and qualitative analysis.* In J.A. Smith, R. Harré, & L. Van Langenhove (Eds.), *Rethinking methods in psychology* (pp.9–26). London, U.K.: Sage.

Stickgold, R., James, L., & Hobson, J.A. (2000). Visual discrimination learning requires sleep after training. *Nature Neuroscience, 3*(12), 1237–1238.

Subject benchmark statement for psychology. (2007). Gloucester, U.K.: Quality Assurance Agency for Higher Education.

Truss, L. (2003.) *Eats, shoots and leaves: The zero tolerance approach to punctuation.* London, U.K.: Profile Books.

Tucker, W. H. (1997). Re-reconsidering Burt: Beyond a reasonable doubt. *Journal of the History of the Behavioral Sciences, 33*(2), 145–162.

Ucros, C.G. (1989). Mood state-dependent memory: A meta-analysis. *Cognition and Emotion, 3,* 139–167.

Yerkes, R. M., & Dodson, J. D. (1908). The relation of strength of stimulus to rapidity of habit formation. *Journal of Comparative Neurology and Psychology, 18,* 459–482.

Zajonc, R.B. (2001). Mere exposure: A gateway to the subliminal. *Current Directions in Psychological Science, 10*(6), 224–228.

Zimbardo, P.G. (1973). On the ethics of intervention in human psychological research: With special reference to the Stanford prison experiment. *Cognition, 2*(2), 243–256.

Index

Terms defined in the Glossary (Appendix 4) have page number in bold type
Statistical terms defined in Appendix 5 have page number in italics
For our website see www.openup.co.uk/psychologysuccess

WHAT TO DO WITH YOUR PSYCHOLOGY DEGREE

Matthew McDonald and Susmita Das

Whether you are planning to pursue a career within the psychology profession or wondering how best to apply the skills you have gained during your psychology studies to another vocation, this practical book will help you to explore the many avenues open to you.

Based on a survey of over 400 UK psychology graduates, *What to do with your Psychology Degree* provides real life information on some of the many occupations and careers open to psychology graduates, ranging from jobs in health, therapy and education to private sector roles in marketing, public relations or the media. By encouraging readers to think laterally about their transferable skills, the authors outline 60 career profiles that are directly and indirectly related to the discipline of psychology. For each occupation the book outlines:

- The main tasks and challenges involved
- Personality attributes that are suited to the job
- Skills needed
- Further training and qualifications that may be required
- Voluntary work placement, part-time, and casual job opportunities
- Links to websites with further information including current vacancies

For any psychology graduate, this book is the most practical resource available on career choices; whether you are embarking on your first job or looking for a change of career, this book is essential reading.

Contents
Introduction – Occupations in mental health and therapy – Occupations in the community – Occupations in education – Occupations in organisations and the private sector – Index.

2008   200pp
978–0–335–22222–3 (Paperback)   978–0–335–22223–0 (Hardback)

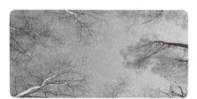